PILLARS of the HOUSE
An Anthology of
VERSE
by
IRISH WOMEN
from 1690 to the present

Edited and selected by A. A. Kelly

1987

WOLFHOUND

Published in Great Britain 1988
First published 1987 in Ireland
WOLFHOUND PRESS
68 Mountjoy Square, Dublin 1.

British Library Cataloguing in Publication Data

Pillars of the House : an anthology of Irish women's poetry.
    1. English poetry — Irish authors
    2. English poetry — Women authors
    I. Kelly, A.A.
    821'.00809287   PR8853

ISBN 0-86327-143-X

This book is published with the assistance of The Arts Council (An
Comhairle Ealaíon), Dublin, Ireland.

Cover illustration: *The Wash House* by William Orpen. By kind permis-
    sion of The National Gallery of Ireland.
Cover design: Jan de Fouw
Typeset by Wendy Commins, The Curragh
Make-up by Paul Bray Studio
Printed by Billings & Sons Ltd.

331378

PILLARS of the HOUSE
An Anthology of
VERSE
by
IRISH WOMEN
from 1690 to the present

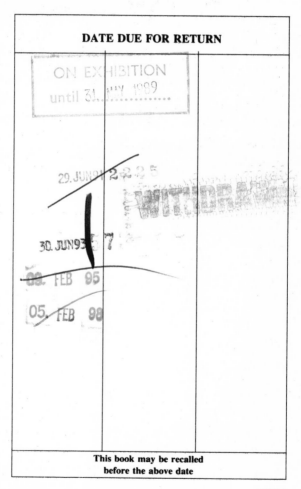

A.A. Kelly was born in London of Irish/Scottish parentage. She has a Doctorate in English Literature and has taught and lectured in Europe and the US. She has ten grandchildren – and her published work includes: (as author) *Mary Lavin: Quiet Rebel* (Wolfhound Press, 1980, paperback edition 1987); *Liam O'Flahery: Storyteller* (Macmillan, 1976); (as editor) *The Pedlar's Revenge & Other Stories* by Liam O'Flaherty (Wolfhound Press, 1976; reissued in paperback as *Short Stories*, 1979). She has co-authored *Joseph Campbell: A Critical Biography* (forthcoming) with Norah Saunders, and is currently preparing a volume of *The Letters of Liam O'Flaherty* for Wolfhound Press.

CONTENTS

8

Acknowledgements

I should like to express particular thanks to the following persons who have been particularly helpful in the compilation of this anthology: Brendan Kennelly (Trinity College, Dublin) for his initial encouragement and advice; James W. Vitty of the Linen Hall Library, Belfast, Michael Longley, Northern Ireland Arts Council, and Nuala Archer, Oklahoma State University, for suggestions and/or information; Maurice Harmon (University College, Dublin) and Eiléan Ní Chuilleanáin (Trinity College, Dublin) for reading the first draft; Joan Trodden Keefe (University of California, Berkeley) and Padraigín Riggs (University College, Cork) for their invaluable help with the Irish language selection and translation.

I am also grateful to all the contributors for their cooperation and forbearance, and to the literary representatives of those poets now dead.

Permission to reprint copyright poems in this anthology is acknowledged with thanks, and apologies offered to those copyright holders whom it has proved impossible to find. We also wish to acknowledge those publishers from whose publications many of these poems have been selected, including The Gallery Press, Raven Arts Press, Beaver Row Press, Arlen House, Blackstaff Press, Coisceim, Sairséal Ó Marcaigh, Cillenna Press, M.H. Gill, Allen Figgis, The Talbot Press, Tempest/ Dundalgan Press, Taxus Press, Faber & Faber, Interim Press, Portmoon Press, Longmans, Smith-Elder, Gayfield Press, Jonathan Cape, Stationery Office, Belfast, Hand & Flower Press, Harry Chambers/Peterloo Poets; also *Hibernia, Cypers, Poetry Ireland Review, The Salmon, Lines Review, The Dublin Magazine, Arena, The Portland Review, Blackwood, The Donegal Democrat, The Irish Times, The Irish Press.*

Introduction

This first anthology of Irishwomen's poetry should enable the reader to follow chronologically the development of such poetry during the past two hundred and fifty years, and to look at the ways in which women's poetry reflects Irish social and political history.

Women's poetry in Ireland was more stringently restricted by contemporary social conditions than men's, for though both sexes suffered from identical politically-imposed limitations, women were also circumscribed by their sex. Women often wrote anonymously. It is known that some of the *Love Songs of Connaught*, first translated by Douglas Hyde, were written by women. Women also wrote many of the popular Irish ballads and are therefore included among what Donagh MacDonagh called 'the submerged body of ballad makers'. How many of these poems and ballads were written by women it is hard to judge as, until the end of the nineteenth century, women continued to write under male pseudonyms, or to use a variety of initials and pen names, only some of which have subsequently been identified.[1]

Louise Bernikov, in her introduction to *The World Split Open* (four centuries of women poets in England and America, 1552-1950) (New York, Vintage Books, 1974; London, The Women's Press, 1979), says: 'The history of women's poetry might be written in terms of the welling up and discarding and welling up again of inhibitions . . . for a woman poet constantly puts herself against expectations of "womanhood" and "women's writing".' This was certainly so until very recently.

Another women's poetry anthology, *The Penguin Book of*

1. Elaine Showalter, in her study of women novelists from Brontë to Lessing, *A literature of their Own* (Princeton University Press 1977; London, Virago 1978), explains the history of women's public image as literary artists.

Women Poets (London, 1978; New York, 1979), editors C. Cosman, Joan T. Keefe and K. Weaver, is international in scope and goes back in time to the fifth century BC. It therefore includes a majority of translations. Among them is the work of three early Irish women poets, two translations from the eighteenth century, and one from the twentieth century, but no Irish poets who wrote in English. The editors, in the Preface to this ambitious anthology, point out that the term 'poetess' rapidly acquired connotations of sentimentality and dilettantism, and that 'the stereotype of the poetess still lingers on into our own time'. The same connotation adheres to 'authoress'. Because of this, say the Penguin anthology editors, some women poets still refuse to allow their work to appear in anthologies devoted exclusively to women. For this anthology no woman I approached refused to contribute for this reason. The Penguin anthology editors also point out that even today there is a tendency to neglect the work of women poets, and that national anthologies include little of their work.

Catherine W. Reilly, editor of the war-poetry anthologies *Scars upon my heart* (1981) and *Chaos of the night* (1984), both from Virago, London, complains that the contribution of women to the poetry of World Wars one and two has been largely ignored. Other major women's poetry anthologies are A. & W. Barnstone's *A Book of Women Poets, from Antiquity to Now* (New York, Schocken Books, 1981); *Bread and Roses*, an anthology of fifty nineteenth and twentieth century women poets (London, Virago 1982), selected and introduced by Diana Scott: the former includes no Irishwomen, and the latter one, Mary Dorcey. There is also *The Bloodaxe Book of Contemporary Women Poets, Eleven British Writers*, ed. Jeni Couzyn (Newcastle-upon-Tyne, Bloodaxe Books, 1985) and *Making for the open: the Chatto book of post-feminist poetry 1964-1984*, ed. Carol Rumens, London: Chatto & Windus (The Hogarth Press) 1985, which includes poets from twenty countries, three from Ireland. The two most recent anthologies of women's work are *The Penguin Book of Australian Women's Poetry*, Victoria 1986, editors Susan Hampton and Kate Llewellyn; and *The Faber Book of Women's Twentieth Century Poetry*, editor Felur Adcock, London 1987 (includes two Irishwomen).

A glance at anthologies of Irish poetry in print show that *The Penguin Book of Irish Verse* (editor Brendan Kennelly) includes six women; *The Faber Book of Irish Verse* (editor

John Montague) includes three women; but *The Oxford Book of Irish Verse* (editor Donagh MacDonagh) was more generous, with seventeen women.[2] Which brings me to the definition of what, for the purposes of this particular volume, being Irish means.

In his 1958 introduction to *The Oxford Book of Irish Verse*, Donagh MacDonagh defines the Irish poet by birth, by descent, by adoption. In this anthology I have excluded poets of Irish descent born outside Ireland, unless they visit or visited Ireland frequently and/or spent most of their life in the country. This excludes Emily Brontë and Nora Hopper, while British Sheila Wingfield, a long-time resident of Ireland and published there, does not wish to be classified as Irish. Included because of their family connection with Ireland, are the two Sheridan granddaughters Caroline Norton and Helen Blackwood, though both were born in London. The only other poets selected who were born and raised outside Ireland are US-born Ivy Bannister and Nuala Archer (both Irish by adoption). It is difficult to know where to draw the line.

All anthologies are necessarily subject to their selector's choice, and others excluded by choice are translators such as Charlotte Brooke, Eleanor Hull, Augusta Gregory and Helen Waddell. Also excluded are Fanny Parnell, Lady Wilde (Speranza), Margaret T. Pender, the Lamont sisters from Belfast who wrote songs set to music, some of *The Nation* poets, the many women who wrote poetry for *Shan Van Vocht*, the elusive Juanita Casey, Agnes Kerr, Freda Loughton and a few others such as Elizabeth Brennan and Eileen Shanahan whom interested readers will find represented in *New Irish Poets*, editor Devin A. Garrity (New York, Devin-Adair, 1948) and *1000 Years of Irish Poetry* (the Gaelic and Anglo-Irish poets from pagan times to the present), editor Kathleen Hoagland (New York, Devin-Adair, 1975).

As both MacDonagh and Montague point out in the introductions to their anthologies, after the Battle of the Boyne (1690) the Gaelic tradition went underground, and the

2. Thomas Kinsella, editor of *The New Oxford Book of Irish Verse* (Oxford University Press 1986), has included no modern women poets. A recent collection of contemporary Irish women's writing including twenty-nine poets and a perspicacious essay by Eavan Boland on 'The Woman Poet, her dilemma' is *Midland Review*, Winter 1986, No. 3, editor Nuala Archer (Oklahoma State University Press).

literary capital of the English language was London. From the eighteenth century the only two named women poets whose work survives in the Irish language are Máire Bhui Ní Laoghaire and Eibhlin Dhubh Ní Chonaill. Ní Laoghaire was illiterate and the texts of her work written down after her death contain so many corruptions that her lament for her son, Seán de Búrc, has regretfully been excluded. Ní Chonaill's 'Lament for Arthur O'Leary' can be found translated into English in most anthologies of Irish poetry. Unfortunately there is only space here for an excerpt from this, one of the great love poems in the Irish language. This Irish poem forms a stark contrast to those of her English-language contemporaries the first of whom, Mary Barber, was appropriately born in 1690. The four other women whose work follows Barber were all born in the eighteenth century. None of their poetry is outstanding but — given the social circumstances of the day — their achievement is remarkable.

Any woman who aspired to become a serious artist at that time was up against it, as the following quotations will show.

Mary Barber, in the preface to the work she was able to publish under Swift's patronage, declares:

'I am sensible that a woman steps out of her province whenever she presumes to write for the Press, and therefore think it necessary to inform my Readers, that my Verses were written with a very different View from any of those which other Attempters in Poetry have proposed to themselves; my Aim being chiefly to form the Minds of my Children . . .'

and she continues in an equally apologetic vein. Swift, in his dedication of her poems to Lord Orrery says:

'. . . she seemeth to have a true poetical genius, better cultivated than could well be expected, either from her sex, or the scene she hath acted in, as the wife of a citizen. Yet I am assured, that no woman was ever more useful to her husband in the way of his business. Poetry hath only been her favourite amusement . . .'

Barber herself recommended the work of Constantia Grierson who, 'was the most excellent scholar, not only in Greek and Roman literature, but in history, divinity, philosophy and mathematics . . . and she acquired this great learning merely by the force of her own genius, and continual application'.[3]

Apart from being largely self-educated, the difficulties of female authors who tried to become serious artists are illustrated by the career of one Elizabeth Ryves, born 1750. Isaac Disraeli, in his *Calamities and quarrels of authors* (edition used 1881), says that Ryves was descended from a family of distinction in Ireland, but was 'deprived of her birthright by the chicanery of the law'. Before this happened she had published 'some elegant odes', a tragedy and comedies, all of which remained in manuscript. Then 'in her distress she took up her pen as a source of existence; and an elegant genius and woman of polished manners commenced the life of a female trader in literature.' Ryves went to London and attempted to live as a literary hack. She was brought 'at length to try the most masculine assertions of the pen. She wrote for one newspaper much political matter' (but never got paid for it), 'much poetry for another' (also unpaid), but 'the most astonishing exertion for a female pen was the entire composition of the historical and political portion of some annual register.' Failing to make both ends meet Ryves next took up translation and taught herself French. She became a competent translator of Rousseau, Raynal, De la Croix and Froissart. Disraeli tells us she lived alone, remained 'virtuous' and died in 'bitter poverty' in 1797. I have selected none of Ryves' work for this anthology, but what was printed before she went to London can be found in her *Poems on several occasions and The Prude*, a comic opera (London 1777). The poems are odes, elegies and pastorals, the spirited work of a young woman. The opera includes many songs. She also wrote one autobiographical novel, *The Hermit of Snowden.*

Isaac Disraeli recommends that those who would know more about the misery of female authors should read what Samuel Whyte has to say. Whyte was Principal of Whyte's Academy, in Grafton Street, Dublin. His pupils included the Duke of Wellington, R.B. Sheridan and Thomas Moore. In Whyte's *A Collection of poems on various subjects* (Dublin 1792), can be found his Epistle IV 'to a lady, soliciting subscriptions to her poems, in answer to a copy of verses on the

---

3. Frances Sheridan, born 1724, mother to Richard Brinsley Sheridan, and a gifted dramatist in her own right, was also self-educated, helped secretly by her brother as her father disapproved of education for women.

occasion.' It is dated October 23rd, 1790. He discourages a certain Henrietta Battier of Dublin from writing and adds:

> And then the sex! ye Gods! on what pretence
> Can they presume to knowledge, wit or sense?
> Flat usurpation! Such a stumbling block
> Must all the lords of the creation shock:
> Not greater was his crime, who durst aspire
> To steal from Heaven great Jove's authentic fire.
> Are there not calls more suited to their parts,
> Domestic cares and culinary arts?
> And if no boys and girls you have to teaze ye,
> Will nothing, cry the Dons, but scribbling please ye?

He tells her that authorship will make her shunned and unpopular, and continued:

> If thou must write and would'st thy works disperse,
> Write novels, sermons, anything but verse:

Women scribblers were tolerated. 'Verse' was the only type of poetry that women, excluded from a classical education, were expected to write, whereas poetry as a serious art form in the eighteenth century depended, of course, on a studied knowledge of poetics based on the classical models, as well as a knowledge of Latin and Greek.

Whyte also gives us some historical anecdotes, and includes an account of his visit to Charlotte Cibber, widowed daughter of the Poet Laureate, Colley Cibber. Like Elizabeth Ryves she was attempting, and failing, to live by her pen, in a thatched cottage in Islington. 'Yet', says Whyte, 'she finished the career of her miserable existence on a dunghill.' This moral tale is supposed to discourage the would-be authoress from branching out on her own, and abandoning the normally dependent feminine role. On the other hand Whyte has clearly formed views on what is wrong with the contemporary education of women, as can be seen from his *The Shamrock or Hibernian Cresses* (Dublin & London 1772), 'a collection of poems, songs, epigrams etc., Latin as well as English, the original production of Ireland, to which are subjoined thoughts on the prevailing system of School Education respecting young ladies, as well as gentlemen, with practical proposals for reformation.'

Whyte says: 'If the female mind be indeed less happily

16

endowed by Nature, stands it not the more in Need of Assistance? If inferior in intrinsic Perfection, does it not the more require Cultivation?' He outlines exactly what is expected of women:

> 'They are the delightful Asylum, the Bosom Friends, and ordained meet Helps to all. The very End of their Creation was for our Happiness, to sweeten our Labours, to alleviate our Cares, to mitigate our Anxieties and our Pains, and to smooth, by the Delicacy of their Manners, and Charms of their Conversation, the rugged Paths of Life. Our Hours of Leisure are their natural Property; and the Conduct of our infant Years, united with our domestic Concerns, their indisputable Prerogative.'

Nevertheless, he continues: 'We avowedly breed them up in Ignorance, and then unjustly and ungenerously accuse and reproach them for the Want of Understanding. Yet the pain they may later take to educate themselves shows that some have both inclination and capacity.' He recommends that women should be given greater opportunity for education, to stop them entering into lives of 'folly, vanity and trifling'. A learned lady is now considered intolerable – 'so conceited! so full of herself', but what, says Whyte, is a learned gentleman but infinitely worse. Whyte complains about the 'custom of smattering' from which women more than men suffer, with their music, French, drawing and writing masters. 'Genius has often showed itself in the poor, despised Country of Ireland: has made noble efforts to expand, and would have produced fruit in due season; but it was nipped in the Bud, and stinted in its growth . . .' and this stricture he finds applies to women even more than to men. Therefore, he concludes: 'Let us give the Minds of our Females a more liberal and proper Bent.' He wants girls to be taught English, geography and history but feels that classics should be left to the more robust intellect of the male. The Irish language, of course, is not mentioned. Whyte had to be careful what he recommended because until as late as the 1880s some doctors held that over-educated girls got atrophied uteruses!

There is another eighteenth century self-taught Irishwoman who must not be forgotten here, though as a translator she is not represented in the anthology, and that is Charlotte Brooke, born 1740, one of twenty-two children, her father Henry being a friend of both Swift and Pope. Brooke is best

17

known for her *Reliques of Irish Poetry* (1789), a collection of Irish poems which she gathered over many years, translated and published. She also wrote a tragedy, *Belisarius*, never printed. Some years after the founding of the Royal Irish Academy Charlotte Brooke petitioned herself to be its housekeeper. She explained that since her father's death she was 'much afflicted' as an unprotected spinster, for her brother had died and with him had gone the inherited income. She had lent some money to a trader who had gone bankrupt. 'I now address myself as a descendant of Genius. I will undertake it, if so required, without a salary.' She calls herself a female orphan. She did not get the post.

Charlotte struggled to get her father's writings republished in a collected edition and died of fever aged fifty-three. What Montague calls her 'spinsterly approach' to the translation of Irish poetry must be viewed in its historical context. It would never have occurred to her much-prized female modesty that she, in her own way, contributed as much, if not more, than her much more famous father to the furtherance of Irish literature. Roger McHugh says of her ('Anglo-Irish poetry 1700-1850', in *Irish Poets in English*, ed. Seán Lucy, Cork & Dublin, Mercier Press 1973): 'This Cavan lady belonged to the Ascendancy but had a real scholar's sense of literary values. Her own translations, although somewhat stilted, sometimes have a poetic force . . . She is rightly honoured as one of a long series of scholars, Irish and English, who helped to bring the ancient treasure of Irish literature into the consciousness of modern poets.'

That a good education helped a woman to achieve is shown by the achievements of Mary Tighe detailed in her biographic notes. She was born the year in which Whyte published his views on women's education. So, for women born at the end of the eighteenth century, it was already becoming easier to write without making the excuses Mary Barber had found necessary. That this was so was due not only to the views of educationalists like Whyte, but also to the efforts of the women themselves. Needless to say, such women had to be socially influential. They also had to be exceptionally energetic, strong-minded, well-educated and not — like most — tied down by a large brood of children.

The remaining two eighteenth century women are both born of Irish fathers and English mothers. Sydney Owenson's (Lady Morgan) *The Wild Irish Girl* (1806) was reprinted seven times in two years. This was the first book to show in popular literary form Ireland's pride in her history and traditions. Augustine Martin notes Walter Scott's debt to Morgan in the early chapters of *Waverley* (A. Martin, in *Anglo-Irish Literature*, Dept. of Foreign Affairs, Dublin 1980, p. 20). Later, when she wrote about her travels in France and Italy, Morgan created protest for her liberal opinions. A great patriot, the Emancipation of Catholics Act of 1829 was in no small part due to the influence of Morgan's novels.

Anna Jameson (née Murphy) was an equally interesting person, though poetry formed a minor part of her literary output, she was an early feminist, writing on the social employment of women, and the relative position of mothers and governesses.

From the nineteenth century there is a large body of work by Irish women poets. By the beginning of the century the Penal Laws had been relaxed, brought about by the effects of the American War of Independence and by pressure from the movement of the United Irishmen and their 1798 rebellion. From 1801 Roman Catholics had the vote (not that this affected women!) but were excluded from Parliament until the Catholic Emancipation Act (1829). Irish women poets played both an active and an important role in the furthering of Irish nationalism.

The Nation (Dublin), a famed political weekly, was begun by supporters of the Young Ireland Movement, Thomas Davis, J.B. Dillon and Charles Gavan Duffy, in 1842. Duffy was arrested and imprisoned after the Young Ireland Rising in 1848, his sister-in-law Margaret Callan taking over his editorial chair. The poets' corner included many female contributors, among them 'Speranza' (Lady Wilde, then Jane F. Elgee, 1824-96, mother of Oscar), a very colourful character; 'Thomasine' (Olivia Knight, Mrs Hope Connolly, c.1830-1909); 'Mary' (Ellen Mary Patrick Downing, 1828-1869), who became Sister Mary Alphonsus of the Presentation Order after her Young Ireland lover had been exiled.

'Speranza's' poetry, excluded here, appears turgid to the modern ear. She promised a leading article after Duffy's arrest and wrote *Jacta alea est* (the die is cast), printed 29 July, 1848. This led to the temporary suppression of *The Nation* by the government, though the paper continued later from 1849-1896 under various editors. Apart from the anonymous 'Bridget', 'Nation' poets selected for this volume are 'Finola' and 'Eva'.

19

Ellen O'Leary, another patriotic poet, was sister to the Fenian John O'Leary. Yeats, in his introduction to the 1892 selection of her work, remarks that her work, and the poetry of J.K. Casey and C. Kickham, made up the whole literary output of the Fenian risings. When in 1864 the Fenians O'Leary, Kickham, Luby and James Stephens were arrested, Ellen was the go-between who ran messages. John O'Leary, found guilty of treason, was imprisoned. Ellen hid rebels and raised £200 on a mortgage to charter a boat for Stephens' escape. In 1867, the Rising having failed, she returned to Tipperary until John completed five years in prison and fifteen years in exile. She then lived with John in Dublin.

Friend and admirer of Ellen was Rose Kavanagh, another patriot. But by the end of the century the mood had changed. Yeats, aged twenty-six when Rose died prematurely, said of her: 'Like most of the best verse in recent years it is meditative and sympathetic, rather than stirring and energetic — the trumpet has given way to the viol and the flute. It is easy to be unjust to such poetry, but very hard to write it. It springs straight out of the nature from some well-spring of refinement and gentleness.'

Had Rose Kavanagh lived longer she might have become as established a poet as her contemporary Katharine Tynan, who lived on to become a 'modern' woman, as the assurance of her 'Any Woman' (from which the title of this anthology comes) shows. Tynan married an Englishman but always wrote under her maiden name. As a young woman she joined the Ladies Land League, but literature, not politics, was her main concern. Her first volume of poems, *Louise de Vallière and other poems* (1885), published with some financial assistance from herself, brought her acclaim and contact with leading figures in the now budding Irish Revival. Her portrait by Jack B. Yeats hangs in the National Gallery, Dublin. She was a joyful, optimistic person.

1866 was a vintage year of birth for Irish women poets. It produced five included here, one of whom died young after childbirth (Frances Wynne). The other Four, Alice Milligan, Ethna Carbery, Dora Sigerson and Susan Mitchell, all produced 'strong and energetic' work quite at variance with Yeats' already quoted comments on the work of Rose Kavanagh.

Women were now better educated. Alice Milligan was not, however, the first university graduate in this anthology (see Ella Young, born 1865). AE (George Russell) believed that

Milligan wrote 'the best patriotic poetry written in Ireland in my time'. Ethna Carbery, Milligan's great friend, was equally patriotic in Northern Ireland at a time when religious affiliation was subordinate to national aspirations. Carbery's work was very popular, called by Seámus MacManus (her husband) 'Ireland's singing handmaiden'. Modern critics dismiss her work as facile and sentimental. This is not always true. A careful scrutiny of her imagery will reveal passion beneath the ladylike veneer, as 'Invocation' shows.

Dora Sigerson was the daughter of doctor/scholar/poet George Sigerson, otherwise 'Erionnach', who became a Senator when aged eighty-six. Dora pre-deceased her famous father. She too wrote poetry full of the love of Ireland. There is a wistfulness about Sigerson's poetry which sets it apart, even from the nineteenth century *fin de siècle* melancholy, and a strong visual imagination. The poems chosen here are not typical of Sigerson the balladeer, but Sigerson the 'lone of soul', exiled by marriage from her country, and by her sex from a physical freedom she evidently craves. The tone of her work is in contrast to that of her friend Katharine Tynan, and her attitude to womanhood in 'A Vagrant Heart' can be compared with Tynan's 'Any Woman'.

The last daughter of 1866, Susan Mitchell, is different again. Much of her work is contemporary satire, hence dated. It includes satires on Dublin personalities, and a parody of 'The Shan Van Vocht' entitled 'The Irish Council Bill 1907' beginning 'Is this what ye call Home Rule!' Her stirring call to 'The Daughters of Erin' is included here to indicate what she felt beneath the *badinage*.

With Mary Devenport O'Neill, though she was born in 1879, we move into the modern era. Women were now permitted, though still often discouraged, from receiving higher education. Much of O'Neill's work, published in *The Dublin Magazine*, remains uncollected.

The word 'sentimental' had previously meant 'refined and elevated feelings', or thought proceeding from emotions and as such, poetry based on 'sentiment' had been considered a peculiarly suitable feminine field. By 1880 its adjectival derivative came to mean 'affected, exaggerated or superficially hackneyed feelings'. These meanings had been creeping in to poetry written by women. Women were still not expected to call a womb a womb, and their 'sentiments' were still expected to be refined.

21

O'Neill attempted to break this stereotype. Unlike many of her predecessors her work is not nationalistically involved, and she does not aim to change the political order. She became Yeats' consultant while he wrote *A Vision* (1925), (see MS 13576 in the National Library of Ireland), and it would be interesting to compare her aesthetic, as revealed in her work, with Yeats' elaborate philosophic system.

Looking back over the poets born in the earlier twentieth century a few interesting facts emerge. Only four poets were born in the 1900-1920 age group, Coghill (primarily a musician), Reynolds (primarily an academic), Lavin (primarily a fiction writer) and Herron (who struggled her way up and was at first an actress). In the next decade there are six poets, Mhac An tSaoi (a barrister, later poet), Strong (primarily a poet but a late starter), Jenkinson, Kelly, Bardwell and Paterson (all late starters). From the thirties come three, Scales and Frost (late starters) and Hartigan (an artist with a large family). It is not until we get to the forties that a dozen poets emerge, all of whom achieved higher education at the right period in their lives, and only three of them, born 1940, 1942 and 1950, (Stanistreet, Cowman, McGuckian) have more than two children. There is a social pattern forming itself here which affected the literary output of these women. Why did so few Irish women write poetry in the age group born 1900-1940?

The reasons are no doubt a complex of social, political and economic factors. Where are the female Kinsellas, Montagues and McFaddens of whom John Jordan says: 'In the twenties were born a quite remarkable group of poets who may be said to form a substantive base of everything that has come since'?[4] Where are the female Lucys, Simmonds, Kennellys and Heaneys, born in the 1930s?

There is only space here to suggest some of the complex reasons for women's reticence, or silence, in Ireland over this period. The development of Eithne Strong's work illustrates some facets of the problem. Her first volume, *Songs of Living* (1961) has a preface by Padraic Colum, in which he says: 'Somewhere in our folk-lore is the Spae-woman: she lives in a lonely hovel in the bog-land or on the mountain-side, and her sayings are enigmatically knowledgeable.'

4. 'Irish Poetry, 1939-1972' in *Irish Poetry Now*, Project Arts Centre, Dublin 1972.

This is somewhat ironic in view of Strong's turbulent houseful! Colum goes on to say:

'We read poetry made by women in the context of poetry made by men. Often we find a defect in women's poetry — it tends to be self-centred, self-regarding, self-pitying. Read C. Rossetti, C.B. Browning, Edna Millay to judge this. But by going back to something ancient Eithne Strong writes of woman's way of life in a way that takes her outside the context that so much of women's poetry has to be read in. We read hers as the utterances of the priestess, the druidess, the sybil . . . her voice has the tone of one who lives outside companies.'

The poetry in Strong's first volume, shows what Colum was getting at. However, Strong's subsequent work has been quite different, and reflects the sociological upheaval she has lived, and is still living, through. *Sarah in Passing* (1974) is a volume of poetry mainly about liberation from domestic tyranny. Her *FLESH . . . The Greatest Sin* (1980) is the female equivalent of Patrick Kavanagh's *The Great Hunger*. For Kavanagh 'Clay is the word and clay is the flesh'; but for Strong, flesh is 'the corruptible mould that grows on bones' and the choice for women in Ireland is between Virgin Nun or Conjugal Rights. The difference in attitude between her 1960 and 1980 poems is immense. Her long *FLESH . . . The Greatest Sin* sequence is objectively self-regarding, but not self-pitying. Here she speaks for all Irish women. The mental or emotional poverty revealed in this work could be compared to the different aspects of poverty shown by Kavanagh, and there are many links between their two points of view. Man was tied to the soil, and woman to her fertile womb. As Kavanagh says, poverty is a mental condition. He considers that his 'The Great Hunger' lacks 'the nobility and repose of great poetry', but he, like Strong, needed to purge himself. That quiet irony, such as one finds in the prose of Irish women writers such as Kate O'Brien, Mary Lavin and, less quietly, in E. Strong, burst its bonds late.

The sociological constrictions on the Irishwoman writer born circa 1910-39 therefore were complex. Though restrictions affected both sexes they bore on women more heavily than on men for the following reasons. Childbearing and rearing remained women's supreme function. Families remained large. For example, the 1926 figures on Irish fertility show that married women under forty-five raised on an average 70% more children than in the USA and 85% more than in England & Wales. The Criminal Law (Amendment) Act 1935 prohibited the sale, advertising, or importation of contraceptives.

Religious loyalties were also paramount. Until the late 1960s the majority of women remained faithful to Church practices, as Terence Brown explains at length in his *Ireland, a Social and Cultural History 1922-1972* (Fontana, London 1981). Women, more straitly than men because of motherhood, were caught up in the religious nets of which Mary Lavin symbolically speaks in her poem included here. A little later Edna O'Brien has voiced the feelings which weighed on the literary woman of the 1950s in her 'Escape to England' (from *Mother Ireland*, Weidenfeld & Nicholson, London 1976).

The Censorship of Publications Acts 1929 and 1946 affected all Irish artists, but married women have less liberty of movement than married men. Until the 1960s there was also considerable legal and social discrimination against women, as well as changing life styles. In 1951, for example, 37% of women worked in agricultural or private domestic service, whereas by 1971 this figure had sunk to 14%. Where had all the maids gone? Who helped with the children? Tillie Olsen's *Silences* (Virago, London 1980) considers the complex issues of creativity versus interruption. 'Where the claims of creation cannot be primary, the results are atrophy; unfinished work; minor effort and accomplishment; silences.'

During this period the equation of large family plus cheap servants, equalling some leisure, gave way to large family minus servants, equalling hard work. Then in the 1960s when the women born in the 1940s reached marriageable age, with increasing prosperity and changing ideas families began to shrink. Ireland still has the highest birthrate in the EEC, but women now have some advantages, compared to the past, from legislation in their favour. At the same time modern technology has entered the home on a scale, and at a price, affordable by the majority, and educational opportunity has improved.

H. H. Richardson, the Australian writer said early in this century that 'almost no mothers – as almost no part-time, part-self persons – have created enduring literature . . . so far.' This is no longer true. Women now have some freedom from compulsory childbearing; technology has replaced servants, though it makes its own demands. But worker/mother/writers are still rare, and when found are parents of small families. Even then this triple role is a most demanding one. W.B. Yeats' poem 'On Woman' (1919) certainly sounds ironic in the modern context:

> May God be praised for woman
> That gives up all her mind,
> A man may find in no man
> A friendship of her kind
> That covers all he has brought
> As with her flesh and bone,
> Nor quarrels with a thought
> Because it is not her own.

Women writers still suffer, to a more extensive degree than their brothers, from what Olsen has called 'the cost of discontinuity'. Olsen (born 1913) says: 'The habits of a lifetime when everything else had to come before writing are not easily broken, even when circumstances now often make it possible for writing to be first; habits of years — response to others, distractibility, responsibility for daily matters — stay with you, mark you, become you.' This may explain why so many of the women are late starters. At what personal, and family, cost younger women are now trying to maintain artistic continuity, or to contain the tensions within the discontinuity, is surely today an important subject for investigation and discussion.

* * * *

The poets born from about 1940 onwards reached adulthood at the time of women's so-called 'liberation'. What are, broadly speaking, the characteristics of these women's poetry?

Pejoratively first, as a still-productive group they are, with some exceptions, open to Colum's criticism. They are often self-regarding, and too conscious of their female function. This is probably an over-reaction, based on strong desire to discuss and reveal previously inhibited experience. Childbirth, a central experience to woman, (see Eavan Boland's 'The Gorgon Head') was until recently a taboo subject. Contraception, rape, abortion and female circumcision are highly emotive and controversial issues about which women find it hard to be objective. The conditioned attitudes towards sex of previous

25

generations, towards subjects still good for a titter, cannot be changed in one generation. Patricia McCarthy in her 'Love-child' and Eiléan Ní Chuilleanáin in her 'Wash' successfully approach delicate matter. Female metaphor is still insecure. Female taboos still permeate the subconscious.

Women poets dare now to write explicitly about their bodies. A glut of this subject, too explicitly expressed, should lessen as female metaphor becomes innate rather than innovative; otherwise there is risk of creating a new stereotype of 'liberated poetess', which would be a disaster.

In some of the younger poets such as Nuala Archer and Medbh McGuckian there is, so far, less obsession with femininity. Archer's 'Whale on the line' is a laconic love poem in the modern mode. McGuckian's 'Gateposts' is serene — less strident than much contemporary work. The younger women's 'voice' is rarely lyrical. They avoid patriotic and religious subjects. They are not primarily concerned with being Irish as such, though, with Máire Mhac An tSaoi leading the way women have begun to write poetry in Irish again. Strong writes in both languages. Maude, Ní Dhomhnaill and Jenkinson's poetic output is only in Irish. Translation or cribs of their work cannot reproduce the flavour of the original to an English language reader.

It is hoped that besides giving a sense of historic perspective this anthology will also help the Irish woman poet to acquire a sense of socio-historic perspective; help her to venture forth and write on wider themes.

Kathleen Raine has defined poetry as: '. . . the language of the soul: . . . its proper function is to create for us images of inner order all share, to open into every present those secret doors, those ways in; to consecrate and redeem for every generation some parcel of the surrounding waste'. (In K. Raine's British Academy Wharton Lecture on English poetry, 'Waste Land, Holy Land', 1976).

In our modern, confused, context, what are the images of inner order we all share? And which parcels of the surrounding waste can Irish women best contribute to redeeming?

A.A. Kelly

MARY BARBER (1690 – 1757)

Married a Dublin tailor. Swift admired her verse and agreed to be her patron, which enabled her to publish by subscription *Poems on Several Occasions* (London 1734), dedicated to John, Earl of Orrery. This was well received but brought her little money, and in 1738 she again appealed to Swift who allowed her to publish his *Polite Conversations*, which sold well. She was also helped by Lady Carteret, wife of the governor general in Ireland.

CONCLUSION OF A LETTER TO THE REV. MR. C –

'Tis time to conclude; for I make it a rule
To leave off all writing, when *Con.* comes from school.
He dislikes what I've written, and says I had better
To send what he calls a poetical letter.
To this I reply'd, you are out of your wits;
A letter in verse would put him in fits;
He thinks it a crime in a woman to read –
Then what would he say should your counsel succeed?

I pity poor *Barber*, his wife's so romantic:
A letter in rhyme! – Why, the woman is frantic.
This reading the Poets has quite turn'd her head!
On my life, she should have a dark room and straw bed.
I often heard say, that *St. Patrick* took care,
No poisonous creature should live in this air:
He only regarded the body, I find;
But *Plato* consider'd who poison'd the mind.
Would they'd follow his precepts, who sit at the helm,
And drive poetasters from out of the realm!

Her husband has surely a terrible life;
There's nothing I dread, like a verse-writing wife:
Defend me, ye powers, from that fatal curse;
Which must heighten the plagues of *for better for worse*!

May I have a wife that will dust her own floor;
And not the fine minx recommended by *More*.
(That he was a dotard, is granted, I hope,
Who dy'd for asserting the rights of the Pope.)
If ever I marry, I'll choose me a spouse,
That shall *serve* and *obey*, as she's bound by her vows;
That shall, when I'm dressing, attend like a valet;
Then go to the kitchen, and study my palate.
She has wisdom enough, that keeps out of the dirt,
And can make a good pudding, and cut out a shirt.
What good's in a dame that will pore on a book?
No! – Give me the wife that shall save me a cook.

27

Thus far I had written — Then turn'd to my son,
To give him advice, ere my letter was done.
My son, should you marry, look out for a wife,
That's fitted to lighten the labours of life.
Be sure, wed a woman you thoroughly know,
And shun, above all things, a *housewifely shrew*;
That would fly to your study, with fire in her looks,
And ask what you got by your poring on books;
Thinking dressing of dinner the height of all science,
And to peace and good humour bid open defiance.

Avoid the fine lady, whose beauty's her care;
Who sets a high price on her shape, and her air;
Who in dress, and in visits, employs the whole day;
And longs for the ev'ning, to sit down to play.

Choose a woman of wisdom, as well as good breeding,
With a turn, at least no aversion, to reading:
In the care of her person, exact and refin'd;
Yet still, let her principal care be her mind:
Who can, when her family cares give her leisure,
Without the dear cards, pass an ev'ning with pleasure;
In forming her children to virtue and knowledge,
Nor trust, for that care, to a school, or a college:
By learning made humble, not thence taking airs,
To despise, or neglect, her domestic affairs:
Nor think her less fitted for doing her duty,
By knowing its reasons, its use, and its beauty.

When you gain her affection, take care to preserve it,
Lest other persuade her, you do not deserve it.
Still study to heighten the joys of her life;
Nor treat her the worse, for her being your wife.
If in judgement she errs set her right, without pride:
'Tis the province of insolent fools, to deride.
A husband's first praise, is a Friend and Protector:
Then change not these titles, for Tyrant and Hector.
Let your person be neat, unaffectedly clean,
Tho' alone with your wife the whole day you remain.
Choose books, for her study, to fashion her mind,
To emulate those who excell'd of her kind.
Be religion the principal care of your life,
As you hope to be blest in your children and wife;
So you, in your marriage, shall gain its true end;
And find, in your wife, a Companion and Friend.

*See Sir Thomas More's *Advice to his Son*.

CONSTANTIA GRIERSON (1706 – 1733)

Lived in Kilkenny and recommended by Mary Barber in her 1734 volume as an entirely self-taught poet and scholar. Barber says of her: 'she was too learned to be vain, too wise to be conceited, too knowing and clear-sighted to be irreligious'. Most of her English poems have been lost. Lord Carteret helped her to get her work published in an anthology, *Poems by Eminent Ladies*, Vol. I (London 1755).

TO MISS LAETITIA VAN LEWEN
(AFTERWARDS MRS. PILKINGTON) AT A COUNTRY ASSIZE

The fleeting birds may soon in ocean swim,
And northern whales thro' liquid azure skim:
The *Dublin* ladies their intrigues forsake;
To dress and scandal an aversion take;
When you can in the lonely forest walk,
And with some serious matron gravely talk,
Of possets, poultices, and waters still'd,
And monstrous casks with mead and cyder fill'd;
How many hives of bees she has in store,
And how much fruit her trees this summer bore;
Or home returning in the yard can stand,
And feed the chickens from your bounteous hand:
Of each one's top-knot tell, and hatching pry,
Like *Tully* waiting for an augury.

When night approaches, down to table sit
With a great crowd, choice meat, and little wit,
What horse won the last race, how mighty *Tray*
At the last famous hunting caught the prey;
Surely you can't but such discourse despise,
Methinks I see displeasure in your eyes:
O my Laetitia, stay no longer there,
You'll soon forget that you yourself are fair;
Why will you keep from us, from all that's gay,
There in a lonely solitude to stay?
Where not a mortal through the year you view,
But bob-wigg'd hunters, who their game pursue
With so much ardour, they'd a cock or hare,
To thee in all thy blooming charms prefer.

You write of belles and beaux that there appear,
And gilded coaches, such as glitter here;
For gilded coaches, each estated clown
That gravely slumbers on the bench has one;
But beaux! they're young attorneys sure you mean!
Who thus appear to your romantic brain.

Alas! no mortal there can talk to you,
That love or wit, or softness ever knew:
All they can speak of's *Capias* and law,
And writs to keep the country fools in awe.
And if to wit, or courtship they pretend,
'Tis the same way that they a cause defend;
In which they give of lungs a vast expense,
But little passion, thought or eloquence:
Bad as they are, they'll soon abandon you,
And gain and clamour in the town pursue.
So haste to town, if ev'n such fools you prize;
O haste to town! and bless the longing eyes
Of *your* CONSTANTIA.

EIBHLÍN DHUBH NÍ CHONAILL (1743 – ?)

One of the twenty-two children of Domhnall Mór O'Connaill of Derrynane, grandfather to Daniel O'Connell, Liberator. First married to an O'Connor, who died six months later, then married Colonel Art O'Leary of the Irish Brigade, and eloped with him against the wishes of her family. They lived near Macroom and, being subject to the Penal Laws as Catholics, her husband could not own a horse worth more than £5. A Protestant neighbour, Morris, offered him £5 for it which in law O'Leary could not refuse. O'Leary challenged Morris to a duel and Morris had him outlawed. The O'Learys, with three young children, were besieged in their house, Eibhlín loading guns for her husband. The soldiers were beaten off and O'Leary escaped but was betrayed by a peasant. He was ambushed and shot in May 1773. His riderless, bloodstained mare brought Eibhlín to his dead body. The lament Eibhlín then composed has become famous, frequently translated into English by poets and scholars such as Seán Ó Cuiv, Seán Ó Tuama, Frank O'Connor, John Montague, Thomas Kinsella, and by Eilis Dillon whose translation has been used here. The lament is, unfortunately too long to include in its entirety. Morris was later shot dead by Art O'Leary's brother.

CAOINEADH AIRT
UÍ LAOGHAIRE

Mo ghrá go daingean tu!
Lá dá bhfaca thu
ag ceann tí an mhargaidh,
thug mo shúil aire dhuit,
thug mo chroí taitneamh duit,
d'éalaíos óm charaid leat
i bhfad ó bhaile leat.

from THE LAMENT FOR
ARTHUR O'LEARY

My love forever!
The day I first saw you
At the end of the market-house,
My eye observed you,
My heart approved you,
I fled from my father with you,
Far from my home with you.

30

Is domhsa nárbh aithreach:
Chuiris parlús á ghealadh dhom,
rúmanna á mbreacadh dhom,
bácús á dheargadh dhom,
brící á gceapadh dhom,
rósta ar bhearaibh dom,
mairt á leagadh dhom;
codladh i gclúmh lachan dom
go dtíodh an t-eadartha
nó thairis dá dtaitneadh liom.

I never repented it:
You whitened a parlour for me,
Painted rooms for me,
Reddened ovens for me,
Baked fine bread for me,
Basted meat for me,
Slaughtered beasts for me;
I slept in ducks' feathers
Till midday milking-time,
Or more if it pleased me.

Mo chara go daingean tu!
is cuimhin lem aigne
an lá breá earraigh úd,
gur bhreá thíodh hata dhuit
faoi bhanda óir tarraingthe;
claíomh cinn airgid,
lámh dheas chalma,
rompsáil bhagarthach —
fír-chritheagla
ar námhaid chealgach —
tú i gcóir chun falaracht
is each caol ceannann fút.
D'umhlaídís Sasanaigh
síos go talamh duit,
is ní ar mhaithe leat
ach le haon-chorp eagla,
cé gur leo a cailleadh tu,
a mhuirnín mh'anama . . . .

My friend forever!
My mind remembers
That fine spring day
How well your hat suited you,
Bright gold banded,
Sword silver-hilted —
Right hand steady —
Threatening aspect —
Trembling terror
On treacherous enemy —
You poised for a canter
On your slender bay horse.
The Saxons bowed to you,
Down to the ground to you,
Not for love of you
But for deadly fear of you,
Though you lost your life to them,
Oh my soul's darling.

Mo chara thu go daingean!
is níor chreideas riamh dod mharbh
gur tháinig chūgham do chapall
is a srianta léi go talamh,
is fuil do chroí ar a leacain
siar go t'iallait ghreanta
mar a mbítheá id shuí 's id sheasamh.
Thugas léim go tairsigh,
an dara léim go geata,
an tríú léim ar do chapall.

My friend you were forever!
I knew nothing of your murder
Till your horse came to the stable
With the reins beneath her trailing,
And your heart's blood on her shoulders
Staining the tooled saddle
Where you used to sit and stand.
My first leap reached the threshold,
My second reached the gateway,
My third leap reached the saddle.

Do bhuaileas go luath mo bhasa
is do bhaineas as na reathaibh
chomh maith is bhí sé agam,
go bhfuaras romham tu marbh
cois toirín ísil aitinn,
gan Pápa gan easpag,
gan cléireach gan sagart
do léifeadh ort an tsailm,
ach seanbhean chríonna chaite
do leath ort binn dá fallaing —

I struck my hands together
And I made the bay horse gallop
As fast as I was able,
Till I found you dead before me
Beside a little furze-bush.
Without Pope or bishop,
Without priest or cleric
To read the death-psalms for you,
But a spent old woman only
Who spread her cloak to shroud you —

do chuid fola leat 'na sraithibh;
is níor fhanas le hí ghlanadh
ach í ól suas lem basaibh.

Your heart's blood was still flowing:
I did not stay to wipe it
But filled my hands and drank it.

Mo chara thu is mo shearc-mhaoin!
Is gránna an chóir a chur ar ghaiscíoch
comhra agus caipín,
ar mharcach an dea-chroí
a bhíodh ag iascaireacht ar ghlaisíbh
agus ag ól ar hallaíbh
i bhfarradh mná na ngeal-chíoch.
Mo mhíle mearaí
mar a chailleas do thaithí.

My friend and my treasure!
It's bad treatment for a hero
To lie hooded in a coffin,
The warm-hearted rider
That fished in bright rivers,
That drank in great houses
With white-breasted women.
My thousand sorrows
That I've lost my companion.

Mó ghrá thu agus mo rún!
Tá do stácaí ar a mbonn,
tá do bha buí á gcrú;
is ar mo chroí atá do chumha
ná leigheasfadh Cúige Mumhan
ná Gaibhne Oileáin na bhFionn.
Go dtiocfaidh Art Ó Laoghaire chugham
ní scaipfidh ar mo chumha
atá i lár mo chroí á bhrú,
dúnta suas go dlúth
mar a bheadh glas a bheadh ar thrúnc
's go raghadh an eochair amú.

My love and my dear!
Your stooks are standing,
Your yellow cows milking;
On my heart is such sorrow
That all Munster could not cure it,
Nor the wisdom of the sages.
Till Art O'Leary returns
There will be no end to the grief
That presses down on my heart,
Closed up tight and firm
Like a trunk that is locked
And the key is mislaid.

A mhná so amach ag gol
sta daidh ar bhur gcois
go nglaofaidh Art Mhac Conchúir deoch,
agus tuilleadh thar cheann na mbocht,
sula dtéann isteach don scoil –
ní ag foghlaim léinn ná port,
ach ag iompar cré agus cloch.

All you women out there weeping,
Wait a little longer;
We'll drink to Art son of Connor
And the souls of all the dead,
Before he enters the school –
Not learning wisdom or music
But weighed down by earth and
stones.

MARY TIGHE (1772 – 1810)

Née Blackford, daughter of the Rev. William Blackford, who died in her second year. Mary's mother was unusual in believing that women needed an education. Governesses were not usual then, so Mrs Blackford taught her French, she had masters for music, drawing and the harp. She later learned Latin from her husband. Her mother became a Methodist and founded the Dublin House of Refuge for Unprotected Female Servants. In 1793 Mary married her cousin Henry Tighe, and spent most of the next eight years in London, where she wrote 'Dissipation'; but Ireland – especially Rosanna, Co. Wicklow, was the place she loved best. Much of her long poem *Psyche, or the Legend of Love* was written there (1801), and the profits from it went to the House of Refuge. By 1805 Mary was ill with tuberculosis, condemned by a doctor to 'the perpetual torture of blisters' back in Ireland. She left diaries detailing her life, and an unpublished novel *Selena*, copied out by hand by her brother-in-law William after her death, and discovered in 1940. Her sonnet 'Written at Killarney' is from p. 536 of volume 5 (National Library of Ireland MS 4746). More information about Mary's last years is in a journal kept by her cousin Caroline Tighe (Mrs Charles Hamilton) (National Library of Ireland MS 4810).

Thomas Moore was her friend and valued her criticism. Mary died in Inistioge, Co. Kilkenny. There was no public sale of her poems until after her death, though in 1805 fifty copies of *Psyche* had been privately printed. *Psyche* was reprinted regularly from 1811-1853.

See Patrick Hench, *The Works of Mary Tighe*, bibliographical society of Ireland, Vol. VI, No. 6, Dublin: At The Sign of Three Candles, 1957; Catherine Jane Hamilton, *Notable Irishwomen*, Dublin: Sealy, Bryers & Walker, 1904; *Keats and Mary Tighe, the poems of M. Tighe with parallel passages from the work of John Keats*, ed. Earle Vonard Weller, New York: Century Co., 1928.

DISSIPATION

Oh! Syren Pleasure! when thy flattering strains
Lured me to seek thee through the flowery plains,
Taught from thy sparkling cup full joys to sip,
And such sweet poison from thy velvet lip,
Didst thou in opiate charms my virtue steep,
Was reason silent, and did conscience sleep?
Oh! let the young and innocent beware,
Nor think uninjured to approach thy snare!
Their surest conquest is the foe to shun;
By fight infected and by truce undone
Secure, at distance, let her shores be past,
Whose sight can poison and whose breath can blast.
Let them not listen to her fatal song
Nor trust her pictures, nor believe her tongue.
Contentment blooms not on her flowing ground,
And round her splendid shrine no peace is found.
If once enchanted by her magic charms,
They seek for bliss in dissipation's arms.
If once they touch the limits of her realm,
Offended principle resigns the helm,
Simplicity forsakes the treacherous shore
And, once discarded, she returns no more.

How soft the pause! the notes melodious cease,
Which from each feeling could an echo call;
Rest on your oars; that not a sound may fall
To interrupt the stillness of our peace:
The fanning west-wind breathes upon our cheeks
Yet glowing with the sun's departed beams.
Through the blue heavens the cloudless moon pours streams
Of pure resplendent light, in silver streaks
Reflected on the still, unruffled lake.
The Alpine hills in solemn silence frown,
While the dark woods night's deepest shades embrown.
And now once more that soothing strain awake!
Oh, ever to my heart, with magic power,
Shall those sweet sounds recall this rapturous hour!

SYDNEY OWENSON (Lady Morgan) (1776 – 1859)

Daughter of a MacOwen from Connaught who anglicized his name. His bankruptcies as a theatrical director affected her education, so did the early death of her mother. Owenson ranks as the first Irish woman novelist after M. Edgeworth. Her *O'Donnel* (1814) was the first novel to have an Irish Catholic hero. She is best known for *The Wild Irish Girl* (1806), for which she studied Irish history and archaeology. She appeals in this bestselling novel for Catholics and Protestants to relinquish their prejudices, and pleads with landlords to spend eight months a year on their estates. She married Sir Charles Morgan three years after this novel came out, and later for fifteen years presided over Dublin's only 'salon'. A tiny, misshapen woman, of great energy and intelligence, she composed 'The Irish Jig' when governess in Co. Tipperary, where she sang and played the harp for forty guests and danced her jig. She was very interested in Irish music. In 1837, as famous author, she was granted an annual pension of £300, and persuaded her husband to move to London.

See Lionel Stevenson's biography, *The Wild Irish Girl*, London: Chapman & Hall, 1936; C.J. Hamilton's *Notable Irishwomen* (1904), pp. 89-103; Colin B. and J. Atkinson's 'Sydney Owenson, Lady Morgan: Irish Patriot and First Professional Woman Writer', *Eire-Ireland* 15, 2, Summer 1980, 60-90.

The poems used here come from *The lay of an Irish harp or metrical fragments*, London: Richard Phillips, 1807.

TO HIM WHO SAID, 'YOU LIVE ONLY FOR THE WORLD'

Oh! no — I live not for the throng
Thou seest me mingle oft among,
By fashion driven.
Yet one *may* snatch in this same world
of noise and din, where one is hurl'd,
Some glimpse of heaven!

When *gossip* murmurs rise around,
And all is empty shew and sound,
Or *vulgar* folly,
How sweet! to give wild fancy play,
Or bend to thy dissolving sway,
Soft melancholy.

When silly beaux around one flutter,
And silly belles gay nonsense utter,
How sweet to steal
To some lone corner (*quite perdue*)
And with the dear elected *few*
Converse and *feel*!

When forced for tasteless crowds to sing,
Or listless sweep the trembling string,
Say, when we meet
The eye whose beam alone inspires,
And wakes the warm soul's latent fires,
Is it not sweet?

Yes, yes, the dearest bliss of any
Is that which midst the BLISSLESS many
So oft *we* stole:
Thou knowst 'twas midst much cold parade
And idle crowds, we each betray'd
To each — a soul.

THE IRISH JIG

Old Scotia's jocund *Highland Reel*
Might make an hermit play the deel!
So full of jig!
Famed for its *Cotillions* gay France is;
But e'en give me the *dance* of *dances*,
An Irish jig.

The slow *Pas Grave*, the brisk *Coupée*,
The Rigadoon, the light Chassée,
Devoid of gig,

35

I little prize; or Saraband
Of Spain; or German Allemande:
      Give me a jig!

When once the frolic jig's begun,
Then hey! for spirit, life, and fun!
      And with some gig,
Trust me, I too can play my part,
And dance *with* all my little *heart*
      The Irish jig.

Now through the mazy figure flying,
With some (less active) partner vying,
      And full of gig;
Now warm with exercise and pleasure,
Each pulse beats wildly to the measure
      Of the gay jig!

New honours to the saint be given
Who taught us first to *dance* to heaven!
      I'm sure of gig,
And *laugh* and *fun*, his soul was made,
And that he often danced and play'd
      An Irish jig.

I think 'tis somewhere clearly proved
That some great royal prophet loved
      A little gig;
And though with warrior fire he glow'd,
The prowess of his *heel* he show'd
      In many a jig!

Nay, somewhere too I know they tell
How a fair maiden danced so well,
      With so much gig,
That (I can scarce believe the thing)
She won a *saint's head* from a *king*
      For one short jig!

But I (so *little* my ambition)
Will fairly own, in meek submission,
      (And with some gig)
That for no HOLY head I burn;
One poor LAY heart would serve MY turn
      For well danced jig.

Since then we know from 'truths divine',
That *saints* and *patriarchs* did incline
      To *fun* and *gig*,
Why let us *laugh* and *dance* for ever,
And still support with best endeavour
      The IRISH JIG.

ANNA BROWNELL JAMESON (1794 – 1860)

Née Murphy, daughter of a United Irishman miniature painter, and an English mother. A prolific writer of prose about travelling in Germany and Canada, Shakespeare's heroines, the social employment of women and legends of the Madonna. The poem chosen here is from *A Lady's Diary* (London: R. Thomas, 1826), published anonymously. It purports to be the work of a fragile and delicate lady who died in her 26th year and is buried in France on the way home. Hence the disillusioned tone of the poem. In reality just before going to Rome as a governess in 1824 Anna had broken off with the Jameson she married the next year. The book, for which Anna got paid ten guineas and a guitar, brought her many friends. According to her etchings in this book Anna was also no mean artist. She did not write much poetry.

See Clare Thomas, *Life of Anna Brownell Jameson* (1967).

LINES

Quench'd is our light of youth!
And fled our days of pleasure,
When all was hope, and truth,
And trusting — without measure.
Blindly we believed
Words of fondness spoken,
Cruel hearts deceived,
So our peace was broken!
What can charm us more?
Life hath lost its sweetness!
Weary lags the hour —
'Time has lost its fleetness!'
As the birds in May
Were the joys we cherish'd,
Sweet — but frail as they,
Thus they pass'd and perish'd!
And the few bright hours,
Wintry age can number,
Sickly, senseless flowers
Lingering through December!

HELEN SELINA BLACKWOOD (Lady Dufferin)
(1807 – 1867)

Née Sheridan, granddaughter of Richard B. Sheridan, daughter of Tom Sheridan. Her mother was widowed and badly off, so Helen and her six siblings were raised in a grace and favour apartment in Hampton Court. She married Price Blackwood, heir to the Marquess of Dufferin. He was in the Navy and away a great deal during their sixteen year marriage (1 son). During her marriage she continued to live with her mother, or in Italy, with frequent visits to her husband's family estate at Clandeboye. After her husband's early death she was courted for years by Lord Gifford (fourteen years her junior). She finally married Gifford just before he died and wrote a very amusing book illustrated by herself, *Lispings from Low Latitudes* (1863), which deserves reprinting. She died of cancer five years later. Meantime her son became High Commissioner of Canada, then Viceroy of India. It was he who edited, with a memoir on the Sheridan family, his mother's *Songs, poems and verses* (London: John Murray, 1894) from which the much-anthologised ballad 'The Irish Emigrant' is taken.

THE IRISH EMIGRANT

I'm sitting on the stile, Mary,
  Where we sat, side by side,
That bright May morning long ago
  When first you were my bride.
The corn was springing fresh and green,
  The lark sang loud and high,
The red was on your lip, Mary,
  The love-light in your eye.

The place is little changed, Mary,
  The day is bright as then,
The lark's loud song is in my ear,
  The corn is green again;
But I miss the soft clasp of your hand,
  Your breath warm on my cheek,
And I still keep list'ning for the words
  You never more may speak.

'Tis but a step down yonder lane,
  The little Church stands near —
The Church where we were wed, Mary —
  I see the spire from here;
But the graveyard lies between, Mary, —

My step might break your rest, —
  Where you, my darling, lie asleep
    With your baby on your breast.

I'm very lonely now, Mary, —
  The poor make no new friends; —
But, oh! they love the better still
  The few our Father sends.
And you were all I had, Mary,
  My blessing and my pride;
There's nothing left to care for now
  Since my poor Mary died.

Yours was the good brave heart, Mary,
  That still kept hoping on,
When trust in God had left my soul,
  And half my strength was gone.
There was comfort ever on your lip,
  And the kind look on your brow.
I bless you, Mary, for that same,
  Though you can't hear me now.

I thank you for the patient smile
  When your heart was fit to break;
When the hunger pain was gnawing there
  You hid it for my sake.
I bless you for the pleasant word
  When your heart was sad and sore.
Oh! I'm thankful you are gone, Mary,
  Where grief can't reach you more!

I'm bidding you a long farewell,
  My Mary — kind and true!
But I'll not forget you, darling,
  In the land I'm going to.
They say there's bread and work for all,
  And the sun shines always there;
But I'll not forget old Ireland,
  Were it fifty times as fair.

And when amid those grand old woods
  I sit and shut my eyes,
My heart will travel back again
  To where my Mary lies;
I'll think I see the little stile
  Where we sat, side by side, —
And the springing corn and bright May morn,
  When first you were my bride.

CAROLINE ELIZABETH SARAH NORTON (1808 – 1877)

Née Sheridan, granddaughter of Richard B. Sheridan, younger sister to Helen S. Blackwood.* Like her sister, Caroline married aged eighteen, both unhappily. Her husband took action against Lord Melbourne, accusing him of relationships with Caroline, and demanding damages of £10,000. He lost the case (1836). She wrote a pamphlet 'English laws for women in the nine-teenth century'. A much admired novelist, no money she earned could legally be hers. The law for her was, she wrote, the same as for the Kentucky slaves. She separated from her husband in 1840, though he continued to make use of her earnings, and took up the cause of criminals and the outcast. The plot of her best novel, *The Lady of La Garaye*, is taken from real life. In 1876 her husband died. She then married Sir William Stirling Maxwell, but died herself three months later. Caroline is 'Diana of the Crossways' in Meredith's novel of that name. The two sonnets printed here come from *The dream and other poems*, London: Henry Colburn, 1841, and reflect her unhappiness before and after separation from her husband.

See Alice Acland's *Caroline Norton*, London: Constable, 1948.

SONNET VI

Where the red wine-cup floweth, there art thou!
Where luxury curtains out the evening sky; –
Triumphant Mirth sits flush'd upon thy brow,
And ready laughter lurks within thine eye.
Where the long day declineth, lone I sit,
In idle thought, my listless hands entwined,
And, faintly smiling at remember'd wit,
Act the scene over to my musing mind.
In my lone dreams I hear thy eloquent voice,
I see the pleased attention of the throng,
And bid my spirit in thy joy rejoice,
Lest in love's selfishness I do thee wrong.
Ah! midst that proud and mirthful company
Send'st *thou* no wondering thought to love and me?

SONNET VII

Like an enfranchised bird, who wildly springs
With a keen sparkle in his glancing eye
And a strong effort in his quivering wings,
Up to the blue vault of the happy sky, –

So my enamour'd heart, so long thine own,
At length from love's imprisonment set free,
Goes forth into the open world alone,
Glad and exculting in its liberty:
But like that helpless bird, (confined so long,
His weary wings have lost all power to soar,)
Who soon forgets to trill his joyous song,
And, feeble fluttering, sinks to earth once more, —
So, from its former bonds released in vain,
My heart still feels the weight of that remember'd chain.

FRANCES BROWN (1816 – 1879)

Born the daughter of a Co. Donegal village postmaster, the
seventh child of twelve. Went blind after smallpox aged
eighteen months. She educated herself by memorising passages
orally from grammar books and dictionaries and developed
an excellent memory. She composed poems from childhood,
first printed in the *Irish Penny Journal* (1840-41) under her
initials, later in *Athenaeum*, and *Chambers Journal*. She dedi-
cated her second volume of poetry to Sir Robert Peel who
after reading her 'The Star of Attéghéi' (1844) had her
awarded an annual pension of £20 from the Royal Bounty.
In 1847 she went to Edinburgh with her sister, determined
to live by her pen. She worked hard, writing reviews, essays,
lyrics and stories, becoming best known for *Granny's Wonder-
ful Chair and other Tales* (reprinted in *The Lucky Bag: Classic
Irish Children's Stories*, Dublin: O'Brien Press, 1984). Her
legends of Ulster appeared in Ulster papers. In 1852, helped
by another well-wisher, Frances moved to London. The poem
chosen here comes from *Lyrics and miscellaneous pieces*,
Edinburgh: Sutherland & Knox, 1848.

SONGS OF OUR LAND

Songs of our land, ye are with us for ever —
    The power and the splendour of thrones pass away;
But yours is the might of some far-flowing river,
    Through Summer's bright roses or Autumn's decay.
Ye treasure each voice of the swift passing ages,
    And truth, which Time writeth on leaves or on sand;
Ye bring us the bright thoughts of poets and sages,
    And keep them among us, old songs of our land!

41

The bards may go down to the place of their slumbers,
    The lyre of the charmer be hush'd in the grave —
But far in the future the power of their numbers
    Shall kindle the hearts of our faithful and brave.
It will waken an echo in souls deep and lonely,
    Like voices of reeds by the summer breeze fann'd;
It will call up a spirit for freedom, when only
    Her breathings are heard in the songs of our land!

For they keep a record of those, the true-hearted,
    Who fell with the cause they had vow'd to maintain;
They show us bright shadows of glory departed,
    Of love that grew cold, and the hope that was vain.
The page may be lost, and the pen long forsaken,
    And weeds may grow wild o'er the brave heart and hand;
But ye are still left, when all else hath been taken —
    Like streams in the desert — sweet songs of our land!

Songs of our land, ye have follow'd the stranger,
    With power, over ocean and desert afar —
Ye have gone with our wanderers through distance and danger,
    And gladden'd their path like a home-guiding star.
With the breath of our mountains in summers long vanish'd,
    And visions that pass'd like a wave from the sand,
With hope for their country and joy for her banish'd,
    Ye come to us ever, sweet songs of our land!

The spring-time may come with the song of her glory,
    To bid the green heart of the forest rejoice —
But the pine of the mountain, though blasted and hoary,
    And the rock in the desert, can send forth a voice.
It is thus in their triumph for deep desolations —
    While ocean waves roll, or the mountains shall stand —
Still hearts that are bravest and best of the nations
    Shall glory and live in the songs of their land!

BRIDGET (anonymous) (c. 1820 – ?)

The poem 'English Schools and Irish pupils' is included here as representative of the many anonymous females whose poetry appeared in *The Nation*, and whose identity remains unknown. It was reprinted in *The Spirit of the Nation, by the writers of The Nation newspaper, being a second series of political songs and national ballads*, Dublin: James Duffy, 1843. 'Bridget' is listed as 'Patricius' in the contents list. This poem also reminds us of the social climate in Ireland at this period.

ENGLISH SCHOOLS AND IRISH PUPILS

from Mrs O'Rorke, formerly Miss Biddy Fudge, to her sister Debby,
in England

Ballysassenagh, March 29, 1843.

I write, my dear Deb., in the greatest distress —
How great it must be you will easily guess,
When I tell you I'm just about bidding adieu
To poor Johnny and Jemmy. I'm sending the two
To England to school. Oh! Debby, my heart
Is ready to break, when I think I must part
My dear darling boys; but its all for their good,
And I'd go through a thousand times more, if I could,
To rear them *genteely* — for ev'ry sensation
Of mine is in favour of *nice* education.
Above all, 'tis the *accent* I'm anxious about;
Good accent's the main point beyond any doubt.
You remember last year how your dear little Kitty
Delighted us all here, her talk was so pretty.
When you asked her to sing about Margery Daw,
And she said with her sweet little frown, '*Au* mamma*u*,'
'Don't a*u*sk me, I pray, sure you know that I *caunt*.'
Had she sung it, she couldn't have more pleased her aunt.
Yes! England's the place for an accent — it's there
One imbibes the pure sounds with the pure English air;
Besides, 'tis the place where a young man will learn
All his mere vulgar Irish attachments to spurn.
While he talks with a tone, he will act with one, too,
That will show he has little with Ireland to do.
Will be thoroughly Englified — shamed out of all
Those nonsensical notions the frize-coated call
Patriotic — will always evince a *sang froid*
That vastly contributes in *my* mind to awe
People into respect; one moves on so *distingue*,
In a path quite apart from the middle-class gangway.
I like a young man with an air supercilious,
Looking English, and aristocratic, and bilious —
It shows folk at once he has rank on his side,
When he looks down on all with a cool, conscious pride.
    Now, Deb., I would ask you, what is there in all
Their language, and science, and stuff that they call
Education at home here that is not vulgarity
Compared with nice manners? — just think what disparity!
    And yet, though fine accent and notions abound
In your Oxford and Cambridge, yet trust me, I found
Poor Mr O'Rorke hard enough to bring round.
He's a good man, indeed — as a husband no better —
Whatever his wife's *bent* on doing — he'll let her;
Minds his lands and his cattle, his markets and fairs;

Talks of rises and falls, and the prices of shares;
In these vulgar affairs he displays some ability,
But not an idea has he of gentility.
Only think how he said th' other day, he'd regret
That his sons were aristocrats — soon was he met
With an answer, I fancy, he'll hardly forget:
'Are your sons like yourself,' said I, 'Mr O'Rorke,
To be noted for knowledge of mutton, and pork?
Fie, for shame on your meanness — I'll *not* be a fool —
I must have my sons sent to England to school —
I'll have none of your brogue — they must speak with an accent,
If all Ballysassenagh were set at a rack rent.
See the Blacks and the Browns — sure my heart it annoys
To see those young fellows look down on our boys;
And why? I'm convinced it's for no better reason,
Than that they were at college in England last season.'
    Thus I argued and fought — above all did I use
Such a tone that I quite beat him out of his views;
So now I'm all tears, and confusion, and racket,
Preparing the boys for the very next packet.
    This being the case, Deb., I'm sure you'll excuse
All mistakes in my hurry to tell you the news;
But whatever my feelings, my fuss, or my fidget,
I am always the self-same, affectionate,

Bridget.

CECIL FRANCES ALEXANDER (1818 – 1895)

Née Humphreys, known as 'Fanny Alexander'. Married to
W. Alexander, from 1850 Archbishop of Armagh and Primate
of All Ireland. Fanny was born in Wicklow and died in Derry.
Her husband was the last Irish bishop to sit in the House of
Lords. She wrote hymns, poems on sacred subjects, memorial
verses, songs for children, narrative and imaginative poems. She
was heavily influenced by Scott, Gray, Byron and Wordsworth.

She is author of such well-known hymns as 'There is a green
hill far away', 'Once in Royal David's city', and 'All things
bright and beautiful'. The two poems chosen here come from
Poems (edited with a preface by W. Alexander), London &
New York: Macmillan, 1896.

DREAMS
(written for children)

Beyond, beyond the mountain line,
The greystone and the boulder,
Beyond the growth of dark green pine,
That crowns its western shoulder,
There lies that fairy land of mine,
Unseen of a beholder.

Its fruits are all like rubies rare,
Its streams are clear as glasses;
There golden castles hang in air,
And purple grapes in masses,
And noble knights and ladies fair
Come riding down the passes.

Ah me! they say if I could stand
Upon these mountain ledges,
I should but see on either hand
Plain fields and dusty hedges:
And yet I know my fairy land
Lies somewhere o'er their edges.

ST. PATRICK'S BREASTPLATE
(written for the Irish Church hymnal based on St. Patrick's 'Lorica'.)
(last two stanzas)

Christ be with me, Christ within me,
Christ behind me, Christ before me,
Christ beside me, Christ to win me,
Christ to comfort and restore me,
Christ beneath me, Christ above me,
Christ in quiet, Christ in danger,
Christ in hearts of all that love me,
Christ in mouth of friend and stranger.

I bind unto myself the Name,
The strong Name of the Trinity;
By invocation of the same,
The Three in One, and One in Three.
Of Whom all nature hath creation:
Eternal Father, Spirit, Word:
Praise to the Lord of my salvation,
Salvation is of Christ the Lord.

MARY EVA KELLY (1825 – 1910)

Known as 'Eva', born Co. Galway of a loyalist father not in
sympathy with the Young Irelanders. Married Kevin Izod
O'Doherty. Well educated, but no formal schooling. Started
writing young and had her first poem, 'The Banshee' published
in *The Nation*, organ of the Young Ireland movement. Kevin
was exiled to Tasmania for his political activities. When he
returned after ten years they married and lived in Paris (1854).
They then returned to Ireland where she wrote ballads and

patriotic verse, and he qualified as a doctor. Later Kevin joined the Irish National Party under Parnell, representing Co. Meath. They finally left Ireland for Queensland, and both died there.

Eva also wrote as 'Fionnuala' in *The Nation*. A biographic sketch of Eva by Justin McCarthy is in *Poems, by 'Eva' of The Nation*, Dublin: M.H. Gill, 1909, (a selected reprint from the 1877 San Francisco published volume of the same title). See D.J. Dillon, 'Eva of *the Nation*', *The Capuchin Annual* (Dublin) 1933, 261-6.

THE PATRIOT MOTHER
A Ballad of '98

'Come, tell us the names of the rebelly crew
Who lifted the pike on the Curragh with you;
Come, tell us their treason, and then you'll be free,
Or right quickly you'll swing from the high gallows tree.'

'*Alanna! alanna!*[1] the shadow of shame
Has never yet fallen on one of your name,
And, oh, may the food from my bosom you drew
In your veins turn to poison if *you* turn untrue.

'The foul words, oh, let them not blacken your tongue,
That would prove to your friends and your country a wrong,
Or the curse of a mother, so bitter and dread,
With the wrath of the Lord — may they fall on your head!

'I have no one but you in the whole world wide,
Yet, false to your pledge, you'd ne'er stand at my side;
If a traitor you lived, you'd be farther away
From my heart, than if true you were wrapped in the clay.

'Oh, deeper and darker the mourning would be
For your falsehood so base, than your death, proud and free —
Dearer, far dearer, than ever to me,
My darling, you'll be on the brave gallows tree.

''Tis holy, *aghra*,[2] from the bravest and best —
Go! go! from my heart, and be joined with the rest;
Alanna machree! O alanna machree![3]
Sure a '*stag*'[4] and a traitor you never will be.'

There's no look of a traitor upon the young brow
That's raised to the tempters so haughtily now;
No traitor e'er held up the firm head so high —
No traitor e'er showed such a proud, flashing eye.

1 My child!   2 My love   3 O child of my heart!   4 an informer

CHARLOTTE GUBBINS (c.1825 – ?)

Née Gibson. Little is known of this poet. 'The Yellow Moon
– Smuggler's Song' is the opening section of a long narrative
poem relating how the poteen-makers get caught, and is con-
tained in *One Day's journal: a story of the revenue police
and other poems*, Sligo: Independent and General Printing
Office, 1862. It is a lively drinking song.

THE YELLOW MOON – A SMUGGLER'S SONG

The yellow moon is clouded, O,
The stars have hid their heads;
The 'boys' are at the brewing, O,
The 'peelers' in their beds;
But let us keep a sharp look out,
For if they knew what we're about,
They'd quickly put us to the rout
          Aye, would they so!

The yellow moon is rising, O,
God bless her when she shines!
She makes our bogs to glimmer bright,
Like far Australia's mines.
And when she peeps beyond the hill
She laughs to see the good old 'still',
And dances round the cup we fill,
          The darlin', O!

The yellow moon is clouded, O,
But she'll shine up by-and-bye;
The 'peelers', too, are in their beds,
But they'll march out presently:
Come, let us drink the work success,
Bad luck to those who wish it less!
And may good fortune ever bless
          The 'Poteen', O!

ELLEN O'LEARY (1831 – 1889)

A native of Tipperary, sister to the Fenian John O'Leary, to
whom she was deeply devoted. Ellen's work was respected by
Yeats, though some of it cloys the modern ear. *The Commercial
Journal, The Irishman* and *The Irish People* helped to spread

her work. Articles about Ellen appeared in *The Irish Monthly*, by Sir Charles Gavin Duffy, and the Rev. Matthew Russell, SJ (Vol. 17, 1889), by Rose Kavanagh and Rosa Mulholland (Vol. 39, 1911). Yeats wrote 'The Poems of Ellen O'Leary', *The Boston Pilot Letter*, 18 April, 1891. Ellen found national feeling her best stimulant to the composition of verse. Her aim was to restore the ballad tradition. The two poems included here come from *The poets and poetry of the century*, Vol. 7 (ed. Alfred H. Miles), London: Hutchinson, 1892. Ellen sometimes used the pseudonym 'Lenel', a transposition of her name.

THE DEAD WHO DIED FOR IRELAND

The dead who died for Ireland;
    Let not their memory die,
But solemn and bright, like stars at night,
    Be they throned for aye on high.

The dead who died for Ireland;
    The noble, gallant Three,
Whose last fond prayer on the gallows' stair
    Was for Ireland's liberty.

The dead who died for Ireland!
    In the lonely prison cell;
Far, far apart from each kindred heart;
    Of their death-pangs none can tell.

The dead who died for Ireland!
    In exile – poor – in pain;
Dreaming sweet dreams of the hills and streams
    They never should see again.

The dead who died for Ireland!
    Let not their memory die,
But solemn and bright, like stars at night,
    Be they throned for aye on high.

A LEGEND OF TYRONE

Among those green hills where O'Neill in his pride,
Ruled in high state, with his fair English bride.
A quaint cottage stood, till swept down by some gale,
And of that vanished home the old wives tell this tale.

* * *

Crouched round a bare hearth in hard, frosty weather,
Three lone, helpless weans cling close together;
Tangled those gold locks, once bonnie and bright,
There's no one to fondle the baby to-night.

'My mammie I want! Oh! my mammie I want!'
The big tears stream down with low wailing chaunt;
Sweet Ely's slight arms enfold the gold head;
'Poor weeny Willie, sure mammie is dead —

And daddie is crazy from drinking all day,
Come down, holy angels, and take us away!'
Eily and Eddie keep kissing and crying —
Outside the weird winds are sobbing and sighing.

All in a moment the children are still,
Only a quick coo of gladness from Will.
The sheiling no longer seems empty and bare,
For, clothed in white raiment, the mother stands there.

They gather around her, they cling to her dress;
She rains down soft kisses for each shy caress,
Her light, loving touches smooth out tangled locks,
And pressed to her bosom the baby she rocks.

He lies in his cot, there's a fire on the hearth;
To Eily and Eddy 'tis heaven on earth,
For mother's deft fingers have been everywhere,
She lulls them to rest in the low *sugaun*[1] chair.

They gaze open-eyed, then the eyes gently close,
As petals fold into the heart of a rose;
But ope soon again in awe, love, but not fear,
And fondly they murmur, 'Our mammie is here!'

She lays them down softly, she wraps them around,
They lie in sweet slumbers, she starts at a sound!
The cock loudly crows, and the spirits away —
The drunkard steals in at the dawning of day.

Again and again 'tween the dark and the dawn
Glides in the dead mother to nurse Willie bawn,[2]
Or is it an angel who sits by the hearth?
An angel in heaven, a mother on earth.

1 rush-seated   2 fair – bán

ELIZABETH W. VARIAN (c.1835 – ?)

Known as 'Finola'. Née Tracy, an early socialist from Co. Antrim. She married the Cork poet Ralph Varian. Her social beliefs are expressed in the poem chosen here, which comes from *Never forsake the ship and other poems*, Dublin: McGlashan & Gill, 1874. This volume contains ballads, simple narrative poems such as 'Only a factory child', and patriotic verse. Finola liked to write about the unsung, convicts, fishermen and simple people. She was a frequent contributor to *The Nation*.

PROUDLY WE STAND IN THE PEOPLE'S RANKS

Proudly we stand in the people's ranks, to war with the people's wrong –
Though not always the race be to the swift, the battle to the strong;
We dare to preach forth the branded creed of equal rights to all –
On the evil and just will the fruitful rain and the cheering sunbeams fall.

Our weapons – true thought and fearless speech – with these we will overthrow
Each low device and base pretence, each aim of the crafty foe;
We laugh at their hollow sophistry, their station, rank, and caste,
Their senseless barricade of words our arms will soon lay waste.

'Tis idle to prate of rank and class – nay urge not the shallow plea –
Remember who sat in the fisherman's boat in Gallilee's (sic) purple sea!
Rend the tyrant chains that custom forged, and recant the impious creed
That a separate law for rich and poor by God's wisdom was decreed.

Remember who sat at the publican's feast! – was there peer or noble there?
What jewelled garter, or diamond star, did those guests, so honoured, wear?
Ah, men arise from delusion's sleep, fling off the coils that bind
The free-born soul's exalted strength, the heaven-endowèd mind,

And proudly stand in the people's ranks, to war with fraud and wrong:
Oh pass not by – ye have stood apart, ye have held aloof too long;
Fear not to utter the glorious faith of equal rights to all:
On the evil and just will the fruitful rain and the cheering sunbeams fall.

ROSA MULHOLLAND (Lady Gilbert) (1841 – 1921)

Born Belfast, a doctor's daughter, married (1891) Sir John
Gilbert, an antiquary. Rosa was educated at home. Dickens
encouraged her early work. Many of her stories were printed
in *Household Words*, and some early novels and articles under
the name of Ruth Murray.

Rosa studied art in London, and contributed to *Cornhill
Magazine*, *The Irish Monthly*, *Duffy's Hibernia Magazine*. She
published her husband's biography in 1905. She was a prolific
novelist. Her three volumes of verse, all published in London
by Elkin Mathews, are *Vagrant Verses* (1886); *Spirit and Dust*
(1908); and *Dream and Realities* (1916).

IN THE GARDEN

Lord, the place is dark with night,
The olive trees are dim to sight;
Scarcely can I see Thee, prone,
Face to earth, outcast, alone.

I have followed Thee with fear,
Followed Thee, and found Thee – here.
Let me cry, and let me pray.
Take the cup of pain away!

Hear me pray and hear me cry
Words of Thine own agony:
Thou the Lord, and God of all;
I, so poor, so weak, so small.

Yet no coward, and if Thou
Urgest this, give courage now!
Calm the shudder at my heart,
Bid my rebel will depart.

Let the measure be filled up,
Filled and drained the bitter cup –
Drained, O Living God, for Thee,
Who hast made this mystery!

HE LAUGHS WHO WINS

Love against Time: and Love hath won the race;
Fly on, fly Time, and pass the trysting place!

Full many a tryst kept we in years agone,
First by a rose-bush, last at a grave-stone.

Fly on, fly Time, and bleach and rend the rose,
That by the crumbling grave-stone buds and blows!

We have been there to meet thee, sorrowing,
Yet now are fled beyond thy swiftest wing.

Fly faster, Time! we laugh at thy delays,
Thou cheat of hearts that fear thy measured days!

We are beyond thy sickle and thy shears;
We have moaned all our pains, shed all our tears.

Thou tyrant art no more; now Love is free
And laughs at Time, safe in Eternity.

EMILY HICKEY (1845 – 1924)

Born Macmine Castle, Co. Wexford, daughter of Canon Hickey.
Co-founder with Dr Furnivall of the Browning Society (1881),
became an academic at Cambridge. English on her father's
side, settled in Ireland from the 17th century, mother from
Co. Carlow. Emily had an Anglo-Irish upper-class upbringing.
Her narrative poems were first printed in *Macmillan's Magazine*.
To her England and Ireland were one and London the great
metropolis. She also wrote early pot-boilers for *Leisure Hour*.
She had a long connection with the newly founded Collegiate
School for Girls in London, lecturing there on English lan-
guage and literature. Emily first became an Anglo-Catholic
and worked in the Christian socialist movement, then a con-
vert to Roman Catholicism in 1901, and close friend of Fr M.
Matthew (*The Irish Monthly* editor). Her *Later poems* were
practically ignored by reviewers because she was involved with
the Catholic Truth Society, and wrote erudite criticism in
Roman Catholic periodicals. She became blind two years
before her death.

See *A Sculptor and other poems* (1889); *Verse tales, lyrics
and translations* (1889); *Michael Villiers, Idealist and other
poems* (1891) and other works. The two poems chosen here
come from *Emily Hickey, poet, essayist, pilgrim*, ed. Enid
Dinnis, London: Harding & More, 1927. There is also an article
about Hickey in *The Irish Monthly*, February 1892.

A ROSE

The sweetest rose it was, the loveliest
   He could in all his garden find:
He brought it, saying, 'Darling, leave your quest
Of knowledge for a little while, and rest
In sweet belief that Nature teaches best.'
   Well did he speak, for, blind
To deep delight that Nature gives, I was
Unquiet-soul'd a seeker for the cause
   Of many a thing and, with cold eyes,
   I sought to read close-folden mysteries,
   Forgetting Love, not Knowledge, maketh wise.

I took his rose and laid it to my mouth.
For one sweet hour I was a girl again,
Forgot my theories form'd at cost and pain,
And all I had gone through for knowledge' sake.
The soul of Eden fragrancy divine
Enter'd this soul of mine
   And quencht its desperate drouth.
It was because I took when Love said '*Take.*'
   My very brow grew smooth
   For drops of spray tost from the Fount of Youth.

      But, woe is me!
I could not let this light and beauty be!
   I pull'd the petals of my rose apart,
With fingers most unkindly tore aside
   The crimson veil that veil'd its golden heart.
I saw the gold, but ah! the flower died.
   And, all unwomanly, in pride,
   'Away with ignorance!' I cried,
   'My flow'rs shall all be knowledge-bringers!
To what availeth joy unless one knows
Its why and wherefore?'

      But my lover sigh'd,
   'Ah, lady, you have kill'd my rose!'
   And his true eyes with unshed tears grew dim,
   Because the voice that had been unto him
Sweetest among the voices of the singers,
On God's good world flung discord's bitter wrong
Instead of sweetest song.

And never now a word of love he speaks,
   But talks of systems and of rules and laws,
   And of effect and cause,
   As learned men talk unto learned men —
And my heart inly breaks,
For oh! to be a woman once again!
So, cruel hand which could such joyaunce slay,

Lay down your pen for aye,
For you will never write those deep-ton'd songs
Of Love and Truth, to live on human tongues,
That human hearts may beat more quick and pure.

But how shall I endure
When One, with sadder eyes than his I griev'd,
Shall look on me whose garden is dead-leav'd?

O ghost of that sweet rose I kill'd,
Wilt thou for ever haunt me night and day?
Must all my life for aye
  With breath of thy dead leaves be fill'd,
And golden dust defil'd cling to the feet
That on thy quivering heart unpitying trod,
And evermore that still, sad voice repeat
That whoso wrongeth Nature wrongeth God.

THE MASTER'S WILL

Thou new-annealed, who in thy love dost ache
To pour out suffering nard-like on His feet,
'Tis great things thou art fain to do; His wheat
Sow, reap, and thresh, nor any wages take;
The stones upon His roadway sit and break;
Panting and thirsty, for the desperate heat,
Or shivering in the heavy wind and sleet;
Only to suffer, suffer for His sake.

And what if thus the Lover of lovers said;
'Not thine the way of brake and tearing brier;
Not thine the torment of the frost and fire;
I give thee gladness, or My passion bred;
I give thee joy; and this is My desire
Thou keep its morning-dew upon thy head'.

EMILY LAWLESS (1845 – 1913)

Eldest daughter of Lord Cloncurry, mother a Kirwan of Co. Galway. A very active woman both physically (swimmer, horsewoman) and mentally, though form was not her strong point. For a good article on her see Edith Sichel in *Nineteenth Century*, July 6, 1914, 80-100. 'A Wave', chosen here, is from *The Inalienable Heritage and other poems*, (privately printed in London 1914). Lady Gregory says of Lawless in her Journal, 'Willy-nilly, landlord's daughter though she might be, child of the land war, she loved every stick and stone of Ireland. She discovered the Aran Islands before Synge'. 'After Aughrim', also included here, is probably her best-known poem. She also wrote historical studies, such as *With Essex in Ireland*; novels, such as *Hurrish* and *Grania*. Her poetry was collected and republished in Dublin in 1965. Professor Wolff's introduction to her reprinted *Traits and Confidences* (Garland 1979), gives a good biographical and critical summary of her work.

A WAVE

Up the long level slope of orbèd earth
Comes this great western wave; now its huge crest
Rims the horizon: now in seeming rest
Onward it comes; no shallow outward mirth
Breaks the calm surface, but below our seeing
Laughs the great heart in ecstasy of being,
Earth and sky respond. The rock-strewn shore
Sounds the approach; down falls its gathered might
Prone on the patient crags and bastions hoar,
Then dies away under the sunset light,
Murmuring 'My task is ended'; murmuring rest
To all the echoing caves. And still the night
Upholds its mantle, and the star-pricked West
Shines hollow; and the hollow pools are white.

AFTER AUGHRIM

She said, 'They gave me of their best,
They lived, they gave their lives for me;
I tossed them to the howling waste,
And flung them to the foaming sea.'

She said, 'I never gave them aught,
Not mine the power, if mine the will;
I let them starve, I let them bleed, –
They bled and starved, and loved me still.'

She said, 'Ten times they fought for me,
Ten times they strove with might and main,
Ten times I saw them beaten down,
Ten times they rose, and fought again.'

She said, 'I stayed alone at home,
A dreary woman, grey and cold;
I never asked them how they fared,
Yet still they loved me as of old.'

She said, 'I never called them sons,
I almost ceased to breathe their name,
Then caught it echoing down the wind,
Blown backwards from the lips of Fame.'

She said, 'Not mine, not mine that fame;
Far over sea, far over land,
Cast forth like rubbish from my shores,
They won it yonder, sword in hand.'

She said, 'God knows they owe me nought,
I tossed them to the foaming sea,
I tossed them to the howling waste,
Yet still their love comes home to me.'

CHARLOTTE GRACE O'BRIEN (1845 – 1901)

Born Cahirmoyle, and never married. She lived in W. Ireland
but travelled to America. She helped in a government scheme
to assist emigrants. A very patriotic woman. Selections from
her writings and correspondence, with a memoir by Stephen
Gwynn (her nephew) were published in Dublin by Maunsel
(1909). The two poems selected here both come from *Lyrics*,
London: Kegan Paul, Trench 1886. 'Hessy' was another
nephew.

HESSY

Goodnight, little Hessy, good-night curly head,
Your eyes are still watching me round,
Though I've tucked you in tight and I've shaded the light,
And there goes the supper-bell's sound.

Goodnight, little Hessy; you've spent the long day
In joy and in brightness and fun;
With your sweet Irish brogue, you dear little rogue,
My foolish soft heart you have won.

56

When I wanted to kiss you, my own little child,
You'd race away quickly from me,
And hide your sweet face in some corner-like place,
Peeping over your shoulder in glee.

Your neck is so fair, and so soft, and so round,
Your eyes are so shaded and quaint,
And the sunbeams they gloss your hair's ruddy toss,
Like the halo around some old saint.

Good-night, little Hessy; God bless you, sweet child,
And keep you your parents' delight;
Now rest you must take, till the morning shall break,
Good-night, little Hessy; good-night.

WICKLOW

O ye Wicklow mountains! 'Golden Spears' of story!
Are your old chiefs forgotten? Are they gone?
Here where fleet-footed once they bounded on,
Followed by their sweet-mouthed hounds — their glory —
In the 'Glen of the thrushes', hot from the chase and gory,
Sweet-mouthed, deep-chested, faithful Brán and Sgéolan.

Erin! Thy children love, and love for ever,
With that abiding love that cannot die,
Thy cloudland, thy mountains, thine ocean, and thy sky,
Thy meadowed valleys green, thy sea-like river,
Can we tear them from our hearts? Can we sever
Those bonds? Ah! never, never — till we die.

MARGARET MARY RYAN (c.1855 – 1915)

Was first published as 'MR' in *The Irish Monthly*, then, not
to be confused with the editor's initials (Matthew Russell),
took the pseudonym 'Alice Esmonde'. She first used her own
name when her poems were collected and published as *Songs
of Remembrance*, Dublin: M.H. Gill, 1889. 'At the Sunset'
comes from this collection of fifty-five poems. Ryan wrote
lyrics and sonnets, often religious in spirit, and dedicated her
verse to the memory of her brother the Very Rev. John Ryan.

AT THE SUNSET

Let us go to the upland shade awhile,
    As the sun sinks down in the crimson west,
See! the fields are lit with a tender smile,
    And the cattle deep in the cool grass rest;

I shall seek this place in the future years,
  I shall know this hour when you're far away;
'Twill be time enough for my grief and tears,
  And I could not weep if I would to-day.

How your hot hand trembles! your face is white,
  And your eyes are strange with the fevered pain,
Like the stars we watched on a late spring's night
  When the death-frost swept over hill and plain:
How the vesper bell thrills the evening air,
  And the silence deepens far and wide!
Our kindred rest in the graveyard there,
  By the tall church tower on the green hill side.

'Tis hard to live, and 'tis hard to die —
  May no troubled dreams on those sleepers break!
God's time is best, and the years go by,
  Yet I know which choice in this hour I'd take.
I remember you as you were a child,
  I can picture since how each bright year ranged,
I can see you young, and glad, and wild,
  I may never know you old or changed.

'Tis a voice of power that has bid you rise,
  And forget your home and your father's land,
To live and die 'neath the stranger's skies,
  And to never clasp but the stranger's hand;
But pain may wait on the unborn years,
  Since pain is best for a human soul,
And the path you chose may be dim from tears,
  When ten thousand waves will between us roll.

Do you think of a morning long ago,
  When the young larks fled through the fields away?
Just a bluer sky and a warmer glow,
  And they took their flight in the bright June day,
With a stronger beat in each parting wing,
  With a joyful tremor they went. Ah! me —
But the heart of man is a weary thing,
  And the ways of God are a mystery.

Will you stand by the seas and behold this place
  As I shall stand when you're far away?
I shall stand in dreams and recall your face,
  As white and strange as it looks to-day.
Will your strong heart pine on the stranger's shore?
  Will your tears flow yet for the friends you leave?
Will you weep for home, should your heart grow sore?
  Will you weep for me, should you learn to grieve?

JANE BARLOW (1857 – 1917)

Born Clontarf, daughter of the Rev. Professor J.B. Barlow, later Vice Provost of Trinity College, Dublin. Died in Wicklow. She was educated at home, later awarded an honorary degree by Trinity. She lived mostly near Dublin and in Wicklow, where she loved to walk the hills. She became a popular writer of poems and sketches of Irish life. She wrote many Irish peasant-life stories, and prose (recently reprinted). The two poems chosen here come from *The Mockers and other verses*, London: George Allen & Sons, 1908 ('The Radiant Frost'); and *Between doubting and daring*, verses, Oxford: B.H. Blackwell, 1916 ('Division', first published in *The Nation*, 1915). Barlow's *Irish Idylls* (London 1892, Cambridge, Mass: Dodd Mead & Co., 1893) had a larger sale than any other contemporary collection of Irish stories. Another volume of verse is *Bogland studies* (1892).

DIVISION

Give Norah Shane, pour soul, who begs her bread,
The penny that she asks,
To bring down showers of blessing on your head
A nimble tongue she tasks;
'Long may ye live, and happy may ye die',
Oft and again I have heard her prayer framed so:
Fared by a week ago . . .

Far lances flash, a bugle's shrill command,
In saddle all his troop;
To let him mount, his mare will hardly stand,
Full gallop off they swoop;
The fretting hooves throb free; he'd think so well
Fay never went; they ne'er fence did ride
In such a glorious run. Down crashed the shell –
No fear! he happy died.

That both should see a whole good wish come true
Was more than Fate could grant.
If Norah's boon thus halved between us two,
One share of joy be scant,
Accept I yet the dole I would fain forego;
Since fair his lot, mine own must needs forgive;
Yea learn alone while days – while hours – creep slow,
How years are long to live.

THE RADIANT FROST

Mist-phantoms wove apace ere night-glooms fled
Their elfin webs of rime, till purelier stoled
Than moon-blanched lilies, glistering fold on fold,
Our frost-charmed wood beneath the dawn rose-red
A splendour grew of spangled boughs dispread
And light-flushed glades, all dazzling to behold,
With gems besprent for dew, for dust clear gold,
From wizard treasuries pearled and diamonded.

Methought: a voice among the undying Dead,
Who saw and sang, the enduring joy hath told
Of even such brief frail beauty. But instead
Came ruffling by a blast of north wind cold,
And wailed withal a word that Shelley said:
Alas then, for the homeless beggar old!

ROSE KAVANAGH (1859 – 1891)

Born Killadroy, Co. Tyrone, educated at Loretto Convent,
Omagh. She first wanted to be an artist and went to the
Metropolitan School of Art, Dublin. An ardent patriot, she
was first published as 'Ruby' in *The Shamrock*, then in *The
Irish Monthly*. She led the youth club in *The Irish Fireside*
and later in *Weekly Freeman*, calling herself 'Remus II'. She
contributed many stories and tales to *Young Ireland* and
other Irish periodicals, but was never published in England.
Much about Kavanagh is contained in a long foreword by
Matthew Russell to *Rose Kavanagh and her verses*, Dublin
& Waterford: M.H. Gill, 1909, from which the two poems
chosen here come. Rose tended Charles Kickham in his final
blindness and deafness. He called her 'Rose of Knockmany'
and wrote a rollicking lyric to her, 'Oh! sure 'tis some fairy'.
Rose died of tuberculosis at Knockmany. Katherine Tynan*
wrote a memorial poem to her, 'My Rose, 'twas the wild rose
you were' and 'Rose in Heaven'.

CHRISTMAS EVE IN THE SUSPECTS' HOME

'Tis Christmas time, my children, the time of peace and mirth;
The ruddy log is blazing on many a happy hearth;
The Christmas lights are burning – the windows all aglow –
But for you and me, my children, this time is a time of woe;
For who will bring the heavy log, with manly strength and pride,
And split it into fragments, and pile them side by side?

60

And who will light the Christmas light, and say the fervent prayer,
That his home and friends and children may in God's protection share,
That neither sin nor sorrow may in his home be found,
And all be safe together when the day again comes round?
And who, my little Mary, shall take you on his knee?
Or laugh to see you toddling round and joining in the glee?
Tonight, my little darling, tonight 'tis sorry cheer,
No merry jokes or fun for us — your father is not here.
I did not miss him half as much until this very night;
The neighbours did the work for us and made our burden light.
But who, tonight, can fill the void that's here in home and heart?
No neighbours, be they e'er so kind, can take tonight his part.
I think I see him sitting in the prison dark and drear,
His eyes are with his heart tonight, and that is surely here.

KNOCKMANY

Knockmany, my darling, I see you again,
As the sunrise has made you a King;
And your proud face looks tenderly down on the plain
Where my young larks are learning to sing.

At your feet lies our vale, but sure that's no disgrace.
If your arms had their will, they would cover
Every inch of the ground, from Dunroe to Millrace,
With the sweet silent care of a lover.

To that green heart of yours have I stolen my way
With my first joy and pain and misgiving.
Dear Mountain! old friend, ah! I would that today
You could thus share the life I am living.

For one draught of your breath would flow into my heart,
Like the rain to the thirsty green corn;
And I know 'neath your smile all my cares would depart
As the night shadows flee from the morn.

AMANDA ROS (1860 – 1939)

Born Co. Down, Anna Margaret McKittrick, married Andrew
Ross, stationmaster of Larne. Trained as a teacher in Dublin.
In 1897 published a novel at her own expense, then two more
novels. Her admirers formed a club which met periodically in
London to exchange quotes from her work. The members
included Lord Beveridge, Robert Lynd, Desmond McCarthy,
E.V. Lucas, F. Anstey, Lord Oxford, and others. Both her
novels and her poetry are eccentric.

See *O Rare Amanda, the life of Amanda McKitterick Ros*, London: Jack Loudan, Chatto & Windus, 1954. In 1944 Denis Johnston presented a short radio biography of her on the B.B.C.

Ros was a satirist. All her work shows up the 'sham and corruption of high society'. She particularly disliked lawyers, clergy and drunks. She remarried a well-to-do farmer when aged sixty-two after her first husband's death. Ros was an ardent Imperialist, a tough, energetic woman who also wrote music and songs, which she sang.

The diatribe against Jamie Jarr included here comes from *Poems of Puncture*, London: Arthur H. Stockwell, 1936. Many of Ros's poems are at the expense of lawyers, and the 'puncture' of the title is intended to deflate lawyers, a metaphorical sticking of a literary pin into the gasbag of litigation. Some of her poetry has a Rabelaisian vigour, in spite of her Victorian prudery. Aldous Huxley called her an Elizabethan born out of her time. During the 1914-18 war she wrote ballads as Monica Moyland and had them printed as broadsheets.

JAMIE JARR

Here lies a blooming rascal
Once known as Jamie Jarr;
A lawyer of the lowest type,
Who loved your name to char.
Of clownish ways and manners,
He aped at speaking fine,
Which proved as awkward to him
As a drawing-room to swine.

I stood while the ground was hollowed
To admit this pile of stink;
They placed the coffin upside down
(The men upon the brink).
How the stony mould did thunder
Upon the coffin's rump,
The fainter grew the rattle
The deeper Jamie sunk.

His mouth now shut for ever,
His lying tongue now stark —
His 'paws' lie still, and never more
Can stab you in the dark.
Earth is by far the richer,
Hell — one boarder more —
Heaven rejoices to be free
From such a legal 'bore'.

KATHARINE TYNAN (1861 – 1931)

Born Dublin, educated St Catherine's Convent, Drogheda until aged only fourteen, married H.A. Hinkson, a barrister, in 1883 and died in England. She lived latterly in Mayo, where her husband was Resident Magistrate. A prolific writer, Tynan's poem 'Any Woman' has given this anthology its title. There is a full bibliography of Tynan's considerable output in *A Bibliography of Modern Irish and Anglo-Irish Literature*, Frank L. Kersnowski, C.W. Spinks, Laird Loomis, San Antonio, Texas: Trinity University Press, 1976.

Tynan was a major poet of her generation, and also widely read by contemporaries for her journalism. Work included here is drawn from *The poems of Katharine Tynan* (ed. Monk Gibbon), Dublin: Allen Figgis, 1963. In 1980 Irish Academic Press published *Twenty One poems* by Tynan.

Interested readers will find Tynan's background outlined by M. Kelly Lynch, with a bibliography, in Robert Hogan's *Dictionary of Irish Literature* (1979). Tynan had three children. She spread her gifts over a wide area (105 novels, 12 short story collections, 18 poetry collections, etc.) as well as being a champion of women's rights. Monk Gibbon calls her 'a patriot but at the same time a citizen of the world', for she travelled and wrote about Europe in her latter years. She also left behind four volumes of memoirs.

ANY WOMAN

I am the pillars of the house;
    The keystone of the arch am I.
Take me away, and roof and wall
    Would fall to ruin utterly.

I am the fire upon the hearth,
    I am the light of the good sun,
I am the heat that warms the earth,
    Which else were colder than a stone.

At me the children warm their hands;
    I am their light of love alive.
Without me cold the hearthstone stands,
    Nor could the precious children thrive.

I am the twist that holds together
    The children in its sacred ring,
Their knot of love, from whose close tether
    No lost child goes a-wandering.

I am the house from floor to roof,
   I deck the walls, the board I spread;
I spin the curtains, warp and woof,
   And shake the down to be their bed.

I am their wall against all danger,
   Their door against the wind and snow,
Thou Whom a woman laid in manger,
   Take me not till the children grow!

WINTER MORNING

The stars faded out of the paling sky,
Dropped through the waters, but the Morning Star
Grew brighter and brighter, and as day was nigh
A pure wind troubled the rushes near and far.

No bird was yet awake: only the duck
Homed to the little lake, fed full with streams:
Strange and unreal the full morning broke
On a still world as God saw it in dreams.

The still-life, austere world was grey and cool,
Lit by one burning torch of purest flame.
Home — from what hidden haunt, what secret pool? —
Borne on the morning wind, the wild duck came.

MARY ANNE HUTTON (1862 – 1953)

Née Drummond, married Arthur William Hutton of Belfast,
a coach-builder. One daughter of the marriage. From a Belfast
Presbyterian family, she was converted to Roman Catholicism
in about 1911. Mary became a Gaelic scholar, and spent ten
years translating *The Táin* freely into English, published by
the Talbot Press, Dublin 1907. The second edition (1924)
was illustrated by Seán MacCathmhaoil. Though decried as
inexact by modern scholars, Hutton's version reads well, as
the excerpt chosen here shows. In appendices she explained
Irish terms, place names, names of persons, tribes and animals,
and the principal sources from which her version of the epic
has been drawn. She says she attempts 'to tell the whole
story of *The Táin* in a complete and artistic form' drawing
from the *Book of Leinster* and the *Yellow Book of Lecan*.
She tried to work like an old shanachie and preserve the Gaelic
spirit of the text.

Then Maev and Al-yill and the hosts of Erin,
Having the bull, fared south; and at the place
Since called the Bressla More on Moy Mweer hevna,
They made their camp at night, having first sent
Their mighty prey in captives and in kine,
And the great bull, the wondrous Dun of Cooley,
Yet farther south, even to Cleer Bo Ulla
For shelter and for safety. And Cucullin
Against the high green grave-hill in the Larguey,
Exceeding near to the great hosts of Erin,
Took up his post; and his own charioteer,
Laeg son of Ree-angowra, kindled there
His fire at eve that night. Cucullin, gazing
Out from himself, perceived the fiery shining
Of their clean gold lance-heads and war-weapons
Above the heads of the Four Fifths of Erin
At falling of the eve that night. He, seeing
Thus the great number of his enemies
And the huge number of his foemen — knowing
Too that his wounds were yet unhealed and yet
He was but weak and feeble — was o'erborne
By rage of anger. He took up his sword,
And his two spears and shield; and shook his shield,
And brandished his two spears, and whirled his sword,
And from his throat he gave his hero-cry,
So that the Bannanahs and Boccanahs,
And the Glen-folk and Spirits of the Air,
Answered him for horror of that cry,
Which thus he raised above him. And the Nowin,
That is to say, the Bive, went through the hosts,
So that the Four Great Fifths of Erin fell
To weapon-trembling; and one hundred warriors
Of the good warriors of the men of Erin
Died of heart-horror 'midst of their camp that night.

MOIRA O'NEILL (1863 – 1955)

Otherwise Agnes Nesta Shakespeare Higginson, born Co. Antrim. Married W.C. Skrine, (their daughter, who writes as M.J. Farrell and as Molly Keane, is a novelist/playwright).

O'Neill's *Songs of the Glens of Antrim*, Edinburgh & London: Blackwood, 1901, were very popular. Much of her poetry is written in dialect, as 'Her Sister' chosen here.

See Hogan's *Dictionary of Irish Literature* for details about her other publications. O'Neill's poetry was collected and published by Blackwood in 1933.

HER SISTER

'Brigid is a Caution, sure!' — What's that ye say?
Is it my sister then, Brigid MacIlray?
Caution or no Caution, listen what I'm tellin' ye . . .
Childer, hould yer noise there, faix! there' no quellin' ye! . . .
Och, well, I've said it now this many a long day,
'Tis the quare pity o' Brigid MacIlray.

An' she that was the beauty, an' never married yet!
An' fifty years gone over her, but do ye think she'll fret?
Sorra one o' Brigid then, that's not the sort of her,
Ne'er a *hate* would *she* care though not a man had thought of her.
Heaps o' men she might 'a had. . . . *Here, get out o' that,*
Mick, ye rogue! deshroyin' o' the poor ould cat!

Ah, no use o' talkin'! Sure a woman's born to wed,
An' not go wastin' all her life by waitin' till she's dead.
Haven't we the men to mind, that couldn't for the lives o' them
Keep their right end uppermost, only for the wives o' them? —
Stick to yer pipe, Tim, an' give me no talk now!
There's the door fore'nenst ye, man! out ye can walk now.

Brigid, poor Brigid will never have a child,
An' she you'd think a mother born, so gentle an' so mild. . . .
Danny, is it puttin' little Biddy's eyes out ye're after,
Swishin' wid yer rod there, an' splittin' wid yer laughter?
Come along the whole o' yez, in out o' the wet,
Or may I never but ye'll soon see what ye'll get!

She to have no man at all. . . . *Musha, look at Tim!*
Off an' up the road he is, an' wet enough to swim,
An' his tea sittin' waitin' on him, there he'll sthreel about now, —
Amn't I the heart-scalded woman out an' out now?
Here I've lived an' wrought for him all the ways I can,
But the Goodness grant me patience, for I'd need it wid that man!

What was I sayin' then? Brigid lives her lone,
Ne'er a one about the house, quiet as a stone. . . .
Lave a-go the pig's tail, boys, an' quet the squealin' now,
Mind! I've got a sally switch that only wants the peelin' now. . . .
Ah, just to think of her, 'deed an' well-a-day!
'Tis the quare pity o' Brigid MacIlray.

NORA TYNAN O'MAHONY (c.1865 – 1932)

Younger sister to Katharine Tynan, she started writing after
her marriage to John O'Mahony, a brilliant barrister who died
aged thirty-three. Her work was published in *The Irish Monthly*
(poetry and stories), in *Ireland Review*, and in the United
States. She wrote one novel, and one children's book.

Poems chosen are from *The Fields of Heaven*, London:
Erskine Macdonald, 1915. Both express loss after her husband's
death.

IN FIELDS OF HEAVEN

As through the meadows green we strolled,
Our little son, but four years old,
With busy hands and tireless feet
Went gathering all the daisies sweet;
Daisies pink-petalled, daisies white,
He gathered them from noon till night.

And as we wandered home at even,
Talking a little while of Heaven,
He, listening, asked with wondering eyes
About this Heaven beyond the skies;
And Daddy answered, with a smile,
'We'll go there in a little while,

'And well I know what you will do
When angels open the door to you!'
'What?' asks the little four-years son.
'To pick God's daisies you will run.'
'And has Heaven fields, and flowers and trees,
And birds, and daisies just like these?'

And Daddy answered, with a smile,
'We'll know, seet – in a little while.'
Oh, little time indeed you stayed!
Even as you spoke I felt afraid.
Darling, 'twas well we could not know
That you would have so soon to go!

But you are gone, and oft at even
I think of you in the fields of Heaven;
And wonder if you lonely are,
Beyond the gleam of moon and star,

For the little child with timeless feet
Who picked all day the daisies sweet,
And if Heaven holds a greater joy
Than a little human, four-years boy.

COMFORTED

As down the winding country road
   I went through wind and rain,
Upon my heart a heavy load
   Of loneliness and pain,
An old man whom I chanced to know,
   In happier days gone by,
Came towards me — white his head as snow,
   And dull and dimmed his eye.

Unconscious there awhile he stood,
   An alms from me to ask,
Peering through eyes beshot with blood
   As though to pierce a mask.
Until swift recognition came
   To light aglow his face;
'Mayrone! and is *he* just the same?
   We missed him round the place!'

But when my black and sombre gown
   Its tale all-grievous told,
The joy from out his face had flown,
   Again 'twas seared and old.
No word of sorrow he let fall,
   Nor tear of mourning shed,
Yet in his eyes I plain read all
   He, tongue-tied, would have said.

As sad and bare of head he went
   Adown the winding road,
Some message seemed from Heaven sent
   To ease me of my load.
For well I knew for whom he prayed —
   Who would not come again —
And I went, strangely comforted,
   Home through wind and rain.

ELINOR MARY SWEETMAN (c.1860 – ?)

Contributed to *The Irish Monthly* as 'E.S.' in 1889/90. Personal details about her seem hard to come by. She published three volumes of verse and lived in Co. Offaly. These are, *Footsteps of the Gods and other poems*, London: George Bell & Sons, 1893; *Pastorals and other poems*, London: J.M. Dent, 1899; *The Wild Orchard*, London: Herbert & Daniel, 1911, from which volume the work here is selected.

THE LOVER'S BREVIARY
At Prime II

Since love is born at last, you say — at last!
Born of us twain —
You wonder that I do not hold him fast —
That I have somehow missed his earliest cry;
After the burden of expectancy,
The burden and the weakness and the pain! —
All these I know. 'Twas I that bore him — I!
And yet,
Now that I hold this child of my desire,
Perfect and beautiful in every limb,
I would awhile forget
What birthtime means to mothers. You are his sire;
O since you fathered him, come, keep him warm —
Close to your bosom clasp his living form; —
I am too faint — I cannot look on him.

AT LAUDS III
To Love the Wanderer
From the Hearth

By what door came you in?
Answer me this.
The walls are high, the portals guarded well,
The roses thorny round my citadel;
The little hidden path is hard to win,
Easy to miss; —
By what door came you in?
Answer me this.

You found a door, you did not even knock,
But on the threshold laughed, and said 'Unlock'
And of itself it fell, and let you through
The guarded way.
Now you are here, — O you, and only you! —
Now you are here, whom all my dreams pursue,
Will you not stay?
O teach me how to hold you lest the stair
On which so lightly now your footsteps beat,
Hereafter should reproach me, saying: *'Where,*
Where are his dearest feet?'
Lest in my empty house the stones cry out,
And all my roses sicken as with drought,
And where your pinions rustled on the floor,
It whispers daily: *'Cometh he no more?'*

Leave me not, Love, — O Love, you will not leave?
Teach me instead how best to fold you in;
How best to make the shutters fast, and weave
My roses thicker where the walls are thin,
Tell me once more, since here you fell on bliss —
O speak, dear prisoner — you must answer this:
How, in my fortress, did you entrance win?
Answer —

ELLA YOUNG (1865 – 1951)

Born Fenagh, Co. Antrim, degree in political science and law
from University College, Dublin. A member of AE's Her-
metical Society, he encouraged her in Irish folklore research.
She lived for months among Connaught peasants learning
Irish, and gathering material. She wrote for *Sinn Féin* and in
1912 rented a Wicklow farmhouse, from where she organised
gun-running for the IRA. She then moved to Achill but
returned to Dublin for 1916, was blacklisted and fled to
Connemara. She returned to Dublin in 1919. In 1925 she
lectured in the United States, settled in California and studied
Mexican and Indian folklore. There she died.

Young is known primarily as a children's writer. See the
article by M. Kelly Lynch in Hogan's *Dictionary* for more
detail here. Her verse was published in Ireland, England, in
New Zealand and American periodicals. Her writing reflects
the influence of the Celtic Revival, in which movement she
had many friends. Poetry chosen here is from *New Songs*, a
lyric selection made by AE from his contemporaries' work,
published Dublin: O'Donoghue, illustrated by Jack B. Yeats,
1903, and in London: A.H. Bullen.

UNTITLED

The sky is silver pale with just one star,
One lonely wanderer from the shining host
Of Night's companions. Through the drowsy woods
The shadows creep and touch with quietness
The curling fern heads and the ancient trees.
The sea is all aglimmer with faint lights
That change and move as if the crystal prow
Of Naive cleft unseen its waveless floor,
And Naive stood there with the magic token,
The apple-branch with silver singing leaves.

70

The wind has stolen away as though it feared
To stir the fingers of her faery mantle
Dream-woven in the land of Heart's Desire:
And all the world is hushed as though she called
Ossian again, and no one answered her.

THE VIRGIN MOTHER

Now Day's worn out, and Dusk has claimed a share
Of earth and sky and all the things that be,
I lay my tired head against your knee
And feel your fingers smooth my tangled hair.
I loved you once, when I had heart to dare,
And sought you over many a land and sea;
Yet all the while you waited here for me
In a still sweetness, shut away from care.
I have no longing now, no dreams of bliss.
But drowsed in peace through the soft gloom I wait
Until the stars be kindled by God's breath;
For then you'll bend above me with the kiss
Earth's children long for when the hour grows late,
Mother of Consolation, Sovereign Death.

ETHNA CARBERY (1866 – 1902)

Pen name of Anna Isabel MacManus, née Johnston, born Bally-
mena, Co. Antrim. She married the poet Seámus MacManus
the year before she died. She wrote many poems for *The
Nation, United Ireland, The Shamrock, Young Ireland, The
Irish Monthly*, etc. Her father, Robert Johnston, was a Belfast
Fenian. In 1894 she founded a monthly, *The Northern
Patriot*, in collaboration with Alice Milligan,* which from
1896-99 was transformed into *The Shan Van Vocht*. Her
volume of poetry *The Four Winds of Eirinn*, Dublin: Gill,
1902, was frequently reprinted, and 'Roddy McCorley goes
to die' became a popular song. Work chosen here comes
from a later collection, *We Sang for Ireland* (poems of E. Car-
bery, A. Milligan and S. MacManus), Dublin: M.H. Gill, 1950.
'Invocation' shows a new assurance from a woman poet.

INVOCATION

The steeds of the Black Wind race
　　Frost-shod and fleet,
Where you hide from my love your face,
　　And stay your feet:

71

In this rose-rimmed quiet glen
   I bide, and pray
     Through the star-filled gloom, and the day,
For your voice again.

The flames on my hearth leap red,
   Each a slender spear;
My bosom awaits your head,
   And to charm your ear
I have wonder-tales without end,
   Fond words untold,
     Or the spell of a harp of gold,
As your wild moods tend.

Oh strong man! man of my love!
   With eyes of dreams,
Pools of the dusk where move
   No starry gleams:
Come from your storm-girt tower,
   Come to my side,
     And sweetly your sheath of pride
Shall break into flower.

When the arrow ends its flight
   You will lonely grow
For a woman's kiss in the night,
   And her breast of snow;
You will reach your arms to the Dark,
   And call and cry
     As the winged winds sweep by —
But no ear shall hark.

THE KISSES OF ANGUS

The kisses of Angus came to me —
And three bright birds on my apple-tree
Pipe their magical haunting song
That shall fill with dreaming my whole life long.

The first bird sings of my love's shut eyes,
The second her lips where silence lies,
The third her blushes for ever fled
And the plenteous curls of her radiant head.

Night and day, asleep or awake,
I carry a heart nigh fit to break,
I carry a pain I shall not forget
Until above me the cairn is set.

For Angus the Druid sent them forth —
These birds that fly to the South and North.
Three kisses he blew on a fateful wind —
These three bright birds for our grief designed.

He bade them circle green Éire round,
Wherever a love-lorn youth he found,
From the High King's son in his torque of gold
To the shepherd guarding his master's fold.

He bade them sting like the honey-bee,
In the bitter-sweet of their minstrelsy;
Or soothe as soft as a mother's croon
When her tired babe droops to the drowsy tune.

He bade them foster the wild unrest
That burns like a flame in a lover's breast,
Or haunt the sad from a burial-place
With the pale content of a ghostly face.

Mo bhrón! mo bhrón! my lady's sleep
Under the bracken is cold and deep;
At head and at foot stands an ogham-stone,
Where my carved lament on each slab is shown.

Why doth the young god hurl his ire
At a lover bereft of his soul's Desire?
My heart goes withering in the sun —
And mirth hath forsaken my father's *dún*.

It is Sorrow's raven I fain would see!
O Angus, call the bright birds from me!
To happier lovers who love may win —
For the hill-fern foldeth my dear one in.

DORA SIGERSON SHORTER (1866 — 1918)

Born Dublin, daughter of the historian George Sigerson, married C.K. Shorter 1895. He was a critic and editor of *The Sphere*, so they lived in England. Douglas Hyde called her 'the greatest mistress of the ballad and the greatest story-teller in verse that Ireland has produced', and George Meredith considered her 'the best ballad writer since Walter Scott'. See Hogan's *Dictionary* for a full bibliography of her prolific output. An obituary of Shorter is in the *Irish Book Lover* IX, Feb/Mar. 1918, 86-7.

A friend of Katharine Tynan* and Alice Furlong* she was an important member of the Literary Renaissance. Work chosen here is from her *Collected Poems*, London: Hodder & Stoughton, 1907, and seems more appropriate than one of her ballads. Those more interested in these could try her *A Legend of Glendalough and Other Ballads*, Dublin & London: Maunsel, 1919.

A VAGRANT HEART

O to be a woman! to be left to pique and pine,
When the winds are out and calling to this vagrant heart of mine.
Whisht! it whistles at the windows, and how can I be still?
There! the last leaves of the beech-tree go dancing down the hill.
All the boats at anchor they are plunging to be free —
O to be a sailor, and away across the sea!
When the sky is black with thunder, and the sea is white with foam,
The grey gulls whirl up shrieking and seek their rocky home.
Low his boat is lying leeward, how she runs upon the gale,
As she rises with the billows, nor shakes her dripping sail.
There is danger on the waters — there is joy where dangers be —
Alas! to be a woman and the nomad's heart in me.

Ochone! to be a woman, only sighing on the shore —
With a soul that finds a passion for each long breaker's roar,
With a heart that beats as restless as all the winds that blow —
Thrust a cloth between her fingers, and tell her she must sew;
Must join in empty chatter, and calculate with straws —
For the weighing of our neighbour — for the sake of social laws.
O chatter, chatter, chatter, when to speak is misery,
When silence lies around your heart — and night is on the sea.
So tired of little fashions that are root of all our strife,
Of all the petty passions that upset the calm of life.
The law of God upon the land shines steady for all time;
The laws confused that man has made, have reason not nor rhyme.

O bird that fights the heavens, and is blown beyond the shore,
Would you leave your flight and danger for a cage to fight no more?
No more the cold of winter, or the hunger of the snow,
Nor the winds that blow you backward from the path you wish to go?
Would you leave your world of passion for a home that knows no riot?
Would I change my vagrant longings for a heart more full of quiet?
No! — for all its dangers, there is joy in danger too:
On, bird, and fight your tempests, and this nomad heart with you!

The seas that shake and thunder will close our mouths one day,
The storms that shriek and whistle will blow our breaths away.
The dust that flies and whitens will mark not where we trod.
What matters then our judging? we are face to face with God.

74

THE LONE OF SOUL

The world has many lovers, but the one
She loves the best is he within whose heart
She but half-reigning queen and mistress is;
Whose lonely soul for ever stands apart.

Who from her face will ever turn away,
Who but half-hearing listens to her voice,
Whose heart beats to her passion, but whose soul
Within her presence never will rejoice.

What land has let the dreamer from its gates,
What face belovèd hides from him away?
A dreamer outcast from some world of dreams,
He goes for ever lonely on his way.

The wedded body and the single soul,
Beside his mate he shall most mateless stand,
For ever to dream of that unseen face —
For ever to sigh for that enchanted land.

Like a great pine upon some Alpine height
Torn by the winds and bent beneath the snow,
Half overthrown by icy avalanche,
The lone of soul throughout the world must go.

Alone among his kind he stands alone,
Torn by the passions of his own strange heart,
Stoned by continual wreckage of his dreams,
He in the crowd for ever is apart.

Like the great pine that, rocking no sweet nest,
Swings no young birds to sleep upon the bough,
But where the raven only comes to croak —
'There lives no man more desolate than thou!'

> So goes the lone of soul amid the world —
> No love upon his breast, with singing, cheers;
> But Sorrow builds her home within his heart,
> And, nesting there, will rear her brood of tears.

IRELAND

> 'Twas the dream of a God,
> And the mould of his hand,
> That you shook 'neath his stroke,
> That you trembled and broke
> To this beautiful land.

Here he loosed from His hold
A brown tumult of wings,
Till the wind and the sea
Bore the strange melody
Of an island that sings.

He made you all fair,
You in purple and gold,
You in silver and green,
Til no eye that has seen
Without love can behold.

I have left you behind
In the path of the past,
With the white breath of flowers
With the best of God's hours,
I have left you at last.

ALICE MILLIGAN (1866 – 1953)

Born near Omagh, Co. Tyrone, educated Methodist College,
Belfast and King's College, London, the daughter of F. Seaton
Milligan, an antiquary. Milligan travelled throughout Ireland
lecturing on Irish history, as a member of the Gaelic League.
With Ethna Carbery*she founded and edited first *TheNorthern
Patriot*, then *Shan Van Vocht* (1896-99). She was later
awarded an Honorary doctorate of literature by the National
University, Dublin. As a patriot of her day Milligan was friends
with O'Donovan Rossa, John O'Leary, Roger Casement. She
was greatly saddened by the division of Ireland in 1922, and
her best work was done before that date. Poems chosen here
are from *Poems*, selected and edited with a lengthy informative
introduction by Henry Mangan, Dublin: Gill, 1954. This
volume also contains an appendix listing the publications in
which Milligan's poetry appeared. Milligan wrote several
plays for the Abbey, among them 'The Last Feast of the
Fianna', the earliest of all Celtic Twilight plays (1900). She
also wrote one novel and a life of Wolfe Tone. See Hogan for
a full bibliography.

Milligan's sister, Charlotte Milligan Fox (d. 1915) founded
the Irish Folk Song Society in 1904. The three poems chosen
here show her skill at ballad writing; her sorrow at the death
of her great friend and collaborator, Ethna Carbery; and her
grief during the Irish civil war.

LORD EDWARD'S WIFE

(*Author's note*: This ballad refers to the laws passed in Edward the Third's reign, in 1366, at Kilkenny, forbidding Norman-Irish nobles to intermarry with the Irish, to keep bards and seanachies, or to use the Irish tongue, on pain of losing life or lands. The date of the events recorded is the time of Richard the Second's invasion, 1394.)

King Richard to the castle rode before the warlike band,
Lord Edward came to greet the King, and stood with cap in hand;
'Now, welcome to my humble roof, come in, my Sovereign Lord,
May heaven confound The Cavanagh, and bless your royal sword.
And take with you the chosen best of these my trainéd men,
They'll guide your armies o'er the moor, or through the mountain glen.'
King Richard from his saddle stept beside the castle door,
And entered to the banquet hall, with fifty knights or more.
The tables groaned with wine, and flesh of oxen and of deer;
Knight Geoffrey mused, 'What lordly woods must yield this lordly cheer.'

The Lady Oona from her bower came forth in silk arrayed,
And low she bowed before the King, her blue eyes gave him welcoming,
    yet not a word she said,
Her hair was black and smooth as silk, and lovely was her face.
'Methinks she comes,' Knight Geoffrey mused, 'of rebel Irish race.'
Beside her stood Lord Edward's heir — a soldier-hearted boy,
For when he saw the knightly arms, his eyes lit up for joy.
Then when the King had sat to eat before Lord Edward's board,
Knight Geoffrey spoke: 'Come hither, child, and look upon my sword.'
The boy stood up beside his knee, and strove the sword to wield,
And stared on ruddy lions, blazed upon the royal shield.
Then in the Irish tongue he told his wonder to the knight,
Who, turning, called unto the King in accents of delight:
'My lord, give ear unto this child, so learned and so young,
Who gives no answer unto me, save in the Latin tongue!'

The King, who lovéd learning well, unto the boy smiled down.
But when he heard the Irish speech, his smile became a frown.
'How comes it that an English boy, and one of lordly race,
Hath dared to speak this rebel tongue before his Sovereign's face?'
He turned where Lady Oona sat, her pale face flushed to red —
Her blue eyes flashed with queenly fire, yet not a word she said.
In anger to Lord Edward then, who sat at his left side —
'And did a Norman noble deign to wed so base a bride?'

Up rose the ancient Seanachie from where he sat below.
His eye was proud, his voice was loud, his beard as white as snow:
'And dared Plantagenet deem base MacCarthy's royal line? . . .
This lady is of nobler race, King Richard, far than thine.
As well the broom might speak in scorn unto the forest king,
When by the summer's smile bedecked with short-lived blossoming.
The oak-tree stands a thousand years, and when at length it falls,

It goes to take the highest place in noble palace halls.
The broom may shine with garb of gold all royally arrayed;
But ere the winds of autumn blow, its blossoms fall and fade,
And then 'tis found a humble plant, for homely uses meet —
High honoured if it sweep the floor for a MacCarthy's feet.'

Oh, wrathful waxed King Richard then, and to the bard he spoke:
'Some guerdon must be granted thee for praising of the oak.
Beside the castle bridge I marked a stout and stately tree;
There thou shalt swing for the scornful words that thou hast dared to me.
Lord Edward, if thou wilt remain a loyal knight of mine,
Send back unto her native bogs this black-haired dame of thine.
And with her send this Irish boy, by English law thou'rt free;
If not, thy house and lands this day are forfeit unto me.
Then bid farewell to Oona here — I'll give three in her place
The loveliest lady of my court, of noble English race.'

The Lady Oona to her lord looked up with trustful pride,
And oh! so tender grew her face, as nobly he replied —
'Oh, dear to me my castle halls, and wealth of wood and wold;
But my marriage-plight and faith as knight cannot be bought for gold.
More precious far than hill or hall, or haunts of dappled deer,
Are the true blue eyes and loving heart of Irish Oona here.
Though loyal to my Sovereign Lord, I'd lay down limb and life,
Mine honour is mine own to keep, with this, my lady wife.'
Then to Knight Geoffrey turned the King, 'These halls are thine to hold,
With every loyal Englishman, and all Lord Edward's gold.'

Across the hills at set of sun Lord Edward rode away —
And he had given house and lands for Oona's love that day.
Her arm was clasped about his waist, her blue eyes shone for joy;
Beside them rode nor squire nor page, but that Irish-speaking boy.
Knight Geoffrey holds the castle walls with Englishmen three score;
But all the Irish kerns are hanged — they'll ride to war no more.
And right above the castle bridge, upon a strong-branched oak,
They hanged the faithful Seanachie for the fearless words he spoke.

THE HOUSE OF THE APPLE TREES
(No. II April 1902)

I was summoned. I am here
With those in all the world to her most dear;
I had no welcome from Her when I came —
No blithe voice from the threshold called my name,
No quick hand drew me in from the rain and wind,
And shut the door behind,
And led me to the warmth of the leaping fire,
Whilst gay eyes sparkled keenly with desire
To hear me tell all 'strange adventures' o'er,
Met since we talked before.

This was Her way of welcome still to me,
Such was our gladness who can never be
So merry any more.
But here is strangest quietness instead;
Low voices — hushed about the lately dead,
Through the long night of waiting where she died,
Whilst the woods roar outside,
And always, always on the window-pane,
Is heard the incessant clamour of the rain
Until the dawn. At dawn
Comes sudden stillness, and I walk upon
The hill-side sloping to the water edge;
And o'er the Abbey of my solemn dreaming
See light of sunrise beaming,
But see no green upon the hawthorn hedge;
The apple-trees upon her garden lawn
Stand gaunt and bare-branched in the shine of dawn,
I know they will be beautiful in May,
But — She has gone away.

TILL FERDIA CAME

We read it in that ancient tale,
The glory of the Northern Gael;
How young Cuchulainn's single sword
Stemmed the advance of Connacht's horde,
And one by one the champions fell
On Ulla's border guarded well;
Battle he deemed a joyous game
Till to the ford Ferdia came.

For as he rested on his blade,
Waiting new contest, undismayed,
Counting the roll of vanquished proudly,
He heard a trumpet challenge loudly,
And from the invading army's rank
A chief strode towards the river bank;
Cuchulainn's hand shook on his sword
As Ferdia faced him at the ford.

Swift on his proud lips died the smile;
('Twas Maeve had planned this deed of guile)
The battle joy that fired his glance
Faded before the uplifted lance
Of Ferdia, his more than brother,
His comrade chosen before all other.
In many a feat of danger tried
And trusted, at Cuchulainn's side
Since boyhood, when each martial sport
They learned at Scathach's island fort;

79

Now to a strife, that was no game,
Against his friend Ferdia came.

Cuchulainn's trust was not betrayed
Spite of the trap Queen Maeve had laid;
To recreant friendship all untender
He steeled his heart — our land's defender
And, after contest long had sped,
He launched at last the gae-bolg dread,
And stricken sore, Ferdia dying,
Clasped in the arms that slew was lying,
Whilst Ulster's champion, bending low,
Uttered his grief in chant of woe,
'Oh, battle was a gladsome game
Till to the ford Ferdia came!'

And in these days of blood and tears
The words re-echo in my ears,
As many a comrade yields his life
To former friend in desperate strife;
I think of Collins in the West,
The life blood clotted on his breast:
And like enough the hand that slew him
Not long before pledged fealty to him,
With many another fighting man
Linked to the cause Republican;
And when through Dublin's street they bore him,
Draping the flag in honour o'er him,
We mourned to think of other days:
His fearless feats, his merry ways.
'Death was a jest, the fight a game
Till to the ford Ferdia came.'

My grief for Childers, Boland too,
And, oh, unconquered Cahal Brugha,
When reeling through the lurid flame
Still armed, defiant still you came
To fall where oft your speech had rung
In accents of our native tongue;
You shed your blood on Dublin street
Where oft, towards festive hall your feet
Had walked in happy company
With lads, who lived this sight to see.
A foreign mandate forced the game
Against Cuchulainn, Ferdia came.

Oh grief! of griefs beyond all other,
Two valiant sons of one fond mother;
Two brothers, pledged to Ireland's righting,
In severed ranks were sternly fighting
In cause opposed: and yet — oh yet

Thank God for this — they had not met.
The deepest, darkest deed of all
Might have befallen — did not befall
Yet — Brian fell by hand of brother
(Some hapless son of Ireland — Mother)
Where battlemented mountains sweep
To end in famed Ben Bulben's steep,
Where Angus raised his cries of woe
O'er the Fianna long ago!
Like Diarmuid wounded by the boar,
When Druid skill could not restore.
His mangled form they brought away
To lay it in Kilbarrack's clay,
And sundered kindred meet to kneel
Above the grave of Brian MacNeill.
As martyr some are praying o'er him,
As erring rebel some deplore him;
No bitterer tears I deem were poured
O'er Ferdia at the Slaughter ford.

Oh brothers! Sons of one loved land,
Who to such combat armed each hand,
What cause of fury and of hate
Had either? By what mocking fate
Are ye, begirt with scornful foes,
Now locked in self-destructive throes,
Whilst they, in calm complacence jeering,
Wait our annihilation nearing;
Wishful that after all your toils,
Of Victory they will reap the spoils.

They tell us in that noble tale,
The glory of the Northern Gael,
When weary of the watch he'd kept
And wounded sore, Cuchulainn slept;
The youth of Erin glad, untired,
With hearts untamed, with hopes inspired,
Rose up against the invading foe.
As it was then it may be so
In these sad days of blood and tears.
Have faith — trust God for happier years,
For strength upheld, for peace restored
'Twixt those who battle at the ford.

FRANCES WYNNE (1866 – 1893)

Born Co. Louth, she married her cousin the Rev. Henry Wynne (1892), and went to East London where he held a curacy. She died eighteen months later after giving birth to a son. Her only volume of verse, *Whisper! and other poems*, London: Elkin Matthews, 1908, has a biographical introduction by Katharine Tynan.* Wynne's poems were published in *Longman's Magazine, The Irish Monthly, Providence Journal* (R.I.), and *The Spectator*.

NOCTURNE

The long day was bright,
It slowly passed from the purple slopes of the hill;
And then the night
Came floating quietly down, and the world grew still.

Now I lie awake,
The south wind stirs the white curtains to and fro.
Cries the corncrake
In fields that stretch by the stream-side, misty and low.

At the meadow's edge
I know the faint pink clover is heavy with dew.
Under the hedge
The speedwell closes its sweet eyes, dreamily blue.

With pursed rosy lips
The baby buds are asleep on the apple tree.
The river slips
Beneath the scarcely swayed willows, on to the sea.

The dark grows, and grows,
But I'm too happy to sleep, and the reason why
No creature knows,
Save certain little brown birds, and my love, and I.

SUSAN LANGSTAFF MITCHELL (1866 – 1926)

Born Carrick-on-Shannon, unmarried, she lived first with the Yeats family in London and then with a sister in Dublin. She was assistant editor to George William Russell (AE) on *The Irish Homestead* and *The Irish Statesman*. Two hundred items are listed under her name in 'A Survey and Index of *the Irish Statesman*', ed. Doyle Smith, University of Washington, 1960.

For more background see Richard M. Kain, *Susan Mitchell*, Lewisburg: Bucknell U.P., 1972, where her uncollected poems are listed.

Mitchell also published work in *The Irish Review* and *Studies*. She was known as a wit for her satires both in verse, and prose. See her mocking study of George Moore's pretensions (1916). She also wrote religious poetry. The poem chosen here comes from *The Living Chalice and other poems*, Dublin & London: Maunsel, 1913, and shows Mitchell's more serious side. Her popular ballad, 'Dermody and Hynes', set to music, can be found in *More Irish Street Ballads*, collected by Colm O Lochlainn, Dublin: Three Candles, 1965; London: Pan, 1978.

TO THE DAUGHTERS OF ERIN

Year after year, from south and north,
    From east and west the tramp of men
Rang on our mother's land, and forth
    To battle marched her sons again.
Year after year we raised the keen
    For heroes of our name and race.
We knelt and wept for what had been,
    All Ireland was a keening place.

The nations saw our mother shamed,
    The nations saw our heads bent low.
Nor knew that in our hearts untamed
    Fire still unquenchable could glow.
With downcast eye and shrouded head,
    Kathleen Ni Houlihan, have we
Showed to the world thy glory fled,
    Our beauty marred betraying thee.

Rise from your knees, O daughters, rise!
    Our mother still is young and fair,
Let the world look into your eyes
    And see her beauty shining there.
Grant of that beauty but one ray,
    Heroes shall leap from every hill,
To-day shall be as yesterday,
    The red blood burns in Ireland still.

EVA GORE-BOOTH (1870 – 1926)

Born Lisadell, Co. Sligo, daughter of Sir Henry Gore-Booth, sister to Countess Constance Markievicz the nationalist. See W.B. Yeats' poem 'In Memory of Eva Gore-Booth and Con Markievicz' (1927). Eva was a social worker in Manchester, where she died, as well as a writer of poetry and verse drama. Though not active in the Irish Literary Revival, she was influenced by it. See Esther Roper's *Poems of Eva Gore-Booth*, with biographical introduction, London: Longman's Green, 1929.

'Comrades' comes from Edna C. Fitzhenry's anthology *Nineteen-Sixteen*, Dublin: Browne & Nolan; London: G.G. Harrap, 1935.

'The Waves of Breffny' is from *New Songs*, AE's anthology of lyrics (1903).

COMRADES

To Con (Constance de Markievicz)

The peaceful night that round me flows,
Breaks through your iron prison doors,
Free through the world your spirit goes,
Forbidden hands are clasping yours.

The wind is our confederate,
The night has left her door ajar,
We meet beyond earth's barréd gate,
Where all the world's wild Rebels are.

THE WAVES OF BREFFNY

The grand road from the mountain goes shining to the sea,
And there is traffic on it and many a horse and cart;
But the little roads of Cloonagh are dearer far to me
And the little roads of Cloonagh go rambling through my heart.

A great storm from the ocean goes shouting o'er the hill,
And there is glory in it, and terror on the wind;
But the haunted air of twilight is very strange and still,
And the little winds of twilight are dearer to my mind.

The great waves of the Atlantic sweep storming on their way,
Shining green and silver with the hidden herring shoal;
But the little waves of Breffny have drenched my heart in spray,
And the little waves of Breffny go stumbling through my soul.

ALICE FURLONG (1875 – 1946)

Born Tallaght, Co. Dublin. Began to publish poetry when aged seventeen, many poems appeared in *The Irish Monthly*, and in the Irish popular press. She also retold stories from old Gaelic literature, collected as *Tales of Fairy Folks, Queens and Heroes*, Dublin: Browne & Nolan, 1907. Her poetry has appeared in a number of anthologies. 'The Rann of Norna' comes from *Roses and Rue*, London: Elkin Mathews, 1899.

THE RANN OF NORNA

I am Norna of the nut-brown tresses,
My home is a hut in the heart of the wood,
Where a fairy footfall the green moss presses,
And high in the branches the grey doves brood;
O sweet comes the wind from the far-off nesses,
Where the sea is a silver and azure flood!

My father is come of Heremon's stock:
He is soft as flour, he is hard as rock.
His blood for his friend, his sword for his foe –
Ah, this pagan law! 'tis a thing of woe.
How shall we plead for pardon, we
Whose sins are the grains of the sands of the sea,
While the ineffaceable words are writ:
'The judgment ye give, ye are judged by it.'

My mother is born of a bardic race,
Amergin looks through her mystic eyes,
Fergus, the Druid, had such a face,
Or Ollav Fodhla, the mighty and wise,
Lore and love in her heart abide.
She is cunning as Mave and kind as Bride.
The wood-doves feed from her milken hand,
She passed the were-wolf by without scathe,
That robbed the graves in Emania's land,
And scattered the bones in its track of death.
Her foster-mother beheld her wraith
Walking the meads on the first of May –
There is in Erin an ancient faith
That whoso is seen hath a long, long day,
If she shall be warm when I am cold,
Blessed be Christ an hundred-fold!

Outside the door of our wattled house
The bee-hives stand in a golden row,
And the hum of the bees is murmurous
From the rose-red dawn till the sun's last glow.

An hundred kine are milked in the dew,
An hundred maids do spin in our hall,
An hundred flocks on the mountain blue
Gather when that our shepherds call,
And an hundred Fenians guard us all.

I am Norna of the nut-brown tresses,
Cathair, my lover is a prince of Saul.
No red stag roams through the wildernesses
With statelier mien than he treads the hall.
His hair is yellow as a leaf in Autumn,
His eyes are bright as the stars in frost,
Virtue and prayer his mother taught him,
His father learned him to lead a host.
He is slow to anger, he is swift to pardon,
He is loth to meddle in contentious strife,
More kind his mouth is, more rich his guerdon
To him who saves than who takes a life.
He is fearless as Daithi in brawl or battle,
Single-handed he fought with a score
When Brian Mac Art stole bard Ethell's cattle —
Brian Mac Art, he stole no more.

They say I am not for a warrior's wife,
That my heart is craven, my spirit weak.
That I shrink from the battle and dread the strife —
Verily 'tis a truth they speak,
For my heart doth sicken at the sight of blood,
And the man turned beast in his savage mood.
O Bards, that sing of the clans out-faring,
And laud the might of the steady stroke,
When brother smites brother with axe unsparing
As the hewer hacks at the senseless oak —
Ye hear but the wind in the banners singing,
Ye hear but the rush of the arrows winging,
Ye see but the glint of the shining steel —
Your brain cannot think, your heart cannot feel!

Columcille, in his passionate youth,
Lifted the sword between North and South.
Sinning he stood on the bloody heath,
The vultures darkened the morning light,
Like a wind went the sob of the hard-drawn breath,
There were ruddy faces gone ashen white,
The hero of the resistless blade
Looked on his work — and was afraid!
Long was his penance, long and sore,
Banished to lone Iona's shore.
Strike for the right, if strike you must.
But glory not in the pride of war;
The body your stroke hath scattered to dust,

You shall answer to God therefor.
See that your battle-cause be just!

Cathair knows that I am no coward,
The blood of Heremon never ran cold.
I climbed the hill when the thick snow showered
To find the lamb that forsook the fold.
Waist-high, I forded the roaring river,
To bring the priest to a dying man,
I tended old Maureen in the plague of fever
When she lay forsaken of her own clan.

I am Norna of the nut-brown tresses,
And I love my lover, the prince of Saul.
I would not part with his kind caresses
To hold all Erin in willing thrall.
One enemy in all Erin I have —
The girl who would wile him away from me;
Yet even her (for Christ's sake) I would save
From death and danger by land or sea.

ELIZABETH SHANE (1877 — 1951)

Born Belfast, real name Gertrude Elizabeth Heron Hine, a
poet, dramatist and musician. Her best known play is 'The
Warming Pan'. Her three volumes of poetry, all published
with contemporary photographs, were collected into two
volumes and revised by J.F. Donovan (of *Irish Bookman*) and
published Dundalk: Tempest, 1945.
    'Off the Rosses' comes from *Tales of the Donegal Coast
and Islands*, London: Selwyn & Blount, 1921; 'Snapdragon'
is from volume two of the collected verse, *Piper's Tunes and
Later Poems*. A poet of nature, the open air, and simple
Ulster folk, Shane's poetry was popular.

OFF THE ROSSES

A soldier's wind in the fairway from the bay to the open sea,
And a boat in at Skull Island that waits for my mate and me;
She is twenty feet from bow to stern and her masts are short and strong,
And with brown sprit-sails on her fore and main, 'tis she can roll along;
With her halyards fast on the weather gun'le, and right good stays are they,
And a bit of a jib to keep her up against she'd make leeway.
O, that is the rig that I would have whenever I go to sea,
For that is the rig of the Rosses man, and it's good enough for me.

Out through the jabble
'Twixt Doonrower and Skull;
Short waves from the cross-tides
Slapping her hull.

Out through the channel
Where the water is deep,
Gliding by banks
Where the broken waves leap;

O, where they laugh and leap,
Tossing their spray,
Close on our weather beam,
A yard away.

Green Inishinny
Is waving with grass;
Grey herons watch us
And stir as we pass.

And it's steady now for the sudden lurch of the waves upon the bar,
And it's up and over them one by one with creaking block and spar,
Till we're clear of them in the open, where the sea is shining grey,
And the breeze is blowing straight and true with nothing to break its way.

We head her north by Umfin and the big rock of Torbane,
And we're through the line of the islands, out west of Inishmeane,
Where the waves come up like mountains with a long unbroken roll,
And the joy of the wide Atlantic makes a plaything of your soul.

O, the boat is stout and steady, and it's what she would need to be;
Her masts are low and her sails are small as she meets each towering sea;
She is like a bird on the white-flecked slope and she takes its joyous lift,
With an easy swing and never a jar to make her ballast shift.

We stay her by Rinogy where the breakers dash and slide,
And it's now for speed with the breeze behind and a boom on either side;
And a steady hand on the tiller as she yaws in the racing sea,
And all hands aft for ballast till we're under the islands' lee.

Then out with the lines and tackle as we make for the fishing ground;
And down with the fores'l to check her speed as we haul and head her
    round
To the bight at the south of Gola where the Mweelmore cliffs stand sheer;
If there's mackerel in the sea at all we'll surely find them here.

All up and down that sheltered mile we have fished full many a day,
With Go and Allagh to the south like jewels in the bay;
And Torglass, a grey sentinel that keeps the ocean's door,
The sternest bit of rock that ever stood on a stormy shore.

O, the jerk and pull of the laden line are things that are good to feel,
And the flash and gleam of the fish as they come are like leaping blades
    of steel;
And the shimmering heap in the boat grows big as the day goes swiftly by,
And the wind works round to the west as the sun is westering the sky.

Out now from the quiet water where the wheeling sea birds call,
And there's time for a reach to the south'ard before the night shall fall;
So we haul a bit to clear the swell on the west of Inishfree,
And then it's a race in a romping breeze to the point of Rinnalea.

The sun is low when we fetch Dunmore, and the breeze falls to an air
As we cross the sandy shallows with all of a foot to spare;
We jibe her there in the channel that is red with the western glow,
And slip along, for the rising tide is under us as we go.

'Tis sweet in the quiet evening, and the moveless waters gleam
As we drift to look for a landing by the edge of a turf-stained stream.
O, peace comes like a crown at last to him who has sought no ease,
And no man loves a haven like the man who has loved the seas.

SNAPDRAGON

I love to see
The honey bee
Alight upon
The snapdragon,
And, hanging, grip
Its under lip,
Pull its mouth wide,
Then slip inside
To steal anew
Of honey dew.
But stealthily those
Lips then close,
Imprisoning
The adventurous thing;
And, even though
He will, I know,
In his own time
With art sublime,
Content and stout,
Squeeze himself out,
I hold my breath
Dreading his death,
That, ere he quit
His thieving, it
One day might hap
Some flaming snap-
Dragon might wake

To thought, and take
Umbrage at the
Marauding bee,
And while he sips
Might snap its lips
With gesture grim,
And swallow him.

MAY MORTON (1876 – 1957)

Born Co. Limerick, full name Mary Elizabeth Morton, lived
in Belfast from 1900 and became secretary, then chairman,
of Belfast PEN. She was a founder member of the Young Ulster
Society. She became Vice-principal of a girls' model school
until 1934. Her verse was published in *Cornhill Magazine*,
Poetry Ireland, *Rann*, etc. She also broadcast on the BBC and
Radio Eireann. Her volumes of poetry are: *Dawn and after-
glow*, Belfast: Quota Press, 1936, and *Masque in Maytime*,
Lisburn: Lisnagarvey Press, 1948 (12 pp). 'Spindle and Shuttle'
won the Festival of Britain Northern Ireland poetry award,
published Belfast: HM Stationery Office, 1951, *Sung to the
Spinning Wheel*, Belfast: Quota Press, 1952 followed. The
poem chosen gives an excellent picture not only of Belfast
weavers but of weaving and spinning, one of the crafts women
over centuries practised – an anonymously produced form of
art to be found now in textile museums, and admired by all.

SPINDLE AND SHUTTLE

Last night I darned a damask tablecloth.

Back and forth
Warp and woof:

The cloth was old; a hundred years and more
Had come and gone since, master of his loom,
Some skilful weaver set the hare and hounds
Careering through the woodland of its edge
In incandescent pattern, white on white.
It was my mother's cloth, her mother's too
(Some things wear better than their owners do)
And linen lasts: a stuff for shirts and shrouds
Since Egypt's kings first built their gorgeous tombs
And wrapped their dead in linen, it may be
They held it symbol of a latent hope
Of immortality.

90

Back and forth
Warp and woof:
Wing of angel,
Devil's hoof.

The glinting needle with its fitful spark,
My Jack o' Lantern on the marsh's dark,
Would pause and shine, would flash and flit along
Divining scene and symbol for a song.

A field of blossomed flax in North Tyrone
Its lean and sheen and shine, its small blue flower
As shy and secret as an Ulster maid
Who saves her smiles like shillings, unaware
Life pays no dividends on thrifty love.

Darning, learning
Yarning, yearning,
Spinning, weaving,
Joying, grieving:

A black flax dam, a field of linen snow,
Linked opposites: the scar upon the soul
Of every Ulsterman. (The spindle turns
And turning winds a thread where clumsy splice
Or stubborn knot will lie upon the spool
To mar the damask's smoothness when the web
Is woven fast.)

Back and forth
Warp and woof:
Wing of angel,
Devil's hoof.

All times make time and all are good and ill;
Twin fibres twist to make the coiling rope
We label time.

And good was twined with ill
When spinning yarn and weaving linen were
Still country crafts. The old blind woman with
Her spinning-wheel beside the open door
Would spin and spin with finger-tips for eyes
Matching the spindle's hunger to her own
Till each was satisfied; but she could feel
The warm sun on her face, the kindly wind
Lay gentle hands upon her faded hair.
The cottage weaver cramped and stiff from toil
That made a convict's treadmill of his loom
Could run a mile around his one green field
To flex his muscles; and could pause a while
To hear the blackbird's song, or sing his own.

Back and forth
Warp and woof:
Wing of angel,
Devil's hoof:

The hand-loom turns to lumber and the wheel
Becomes a thing to win a tourist's glance
When far from field and bird the factories rise,
A myriad spindles and a maze of looms
Cradled within four walls. On every side
Thin streets of small brick houses spawn and sprawl
Though none could give its neighbour elbow-room.
Sleep flies each morning at the siren's shout
And women hurry, shapeless in their shawls,
In multitudes made nameless, to the mill,
Some young, some old, and many great with child:
All wage slaves of the new industrial age,
All temple vestals of the linen god.
Some will put off their shoes from off their feet
And barefoot serve the spindles all day long,
Some will keep constant vigil where the looms
Like giant nightmare spiders pounce and crawl
With spider skill across the tethered web
While captive shuttles darting to and fro
Will weave, not hare and hounds, but shamrock sprays
To tempt nostalgic exiles. None may rest
Till day ends and the siren sets them free.
Even the children, sad as wilting flowers
Plucked in the bud, must give their days to toil,
Their nights to weariness and never know
How morning comes with laughter to a child.
But linen prospers and the linen lords
Build fine town mansions for their families
And plan a city hall whose splendid dome
Will soar above the long lean streets and look
Beyond them to the green encircling hills.

Back and forth
Warp and woof:
Wing of angel,
Devil's hoof:

Young men see visions and old men dream dreams:
Their beacons lit on summits far away,
Their faith entangled in the baffling rope,
Good twined with evil, evil twined with good.
Strand upon strand with whiter strands for some;
The spinner and the weaver in the mill
Now earn a living and have time to live,
Children whose mothers were half-timers once
Untouchables in factory and school

May learn to play and even play to learn
And think of spindle as a word to spell.
Mill-girls have shed their shawl-cocoons and shine
Brighter than butterflies. With gleaming hair
And ankles neat in nylon each can look
Into her mirror with a practised smile
And see herself the reigning linen queen.
The great domed hall four-square in stubborn stone
With polished marble floors magnificent
As any Rajah's palace has stood now
For nearly half a century. Strange how
The little laurel hedge that hems its lawns
Reveals we still are country-folk at heart
Deep-rooted in the fields our fathers tilled.

       Back and forth
       Warp and woof:
       Wing of angel,
       Devil's hoof:

The white strands catch the moment's light, and show
A pattern in the fabric, damask smooth.
We spin and weave, with yarns and years and tears
Our webs of linen and of destiny:
A people's life is netted in the loom
Their story echoes in the spindle's song.
Through slump to boom, through war to peace — this peace
The frightened hare with hounds upon her track
Running to meet the terror that she flees.

       Darning, dreaming,
       Thinking long,
   Flax and flux and wheel and song;
       Good and evil,
       Right and wrong.

Spend and lend and buy and borrow,
Yesterday, to-day, to-morrow:
       Weaving linen,
       Spinning thread,
Weaving guns and spinning bread;
       Sheets and shrouds
       And shirts and collars
Earning dollars, dollars, dollars!

See how fast the wheels are turning:
Rome is burning, burning, burning!
Hear the crying of the fiddle:
Hands across and up the middle
Choose your partners for the dance
Weave your webs or take your chance!

Hear the clatter of the loom:
Atom bomb and day of doom!
Will the clatter never cease?
Work for war and hope for peace.
Hear the spindle's gentler hum:
Work for peace and peace may come.

In fields of North Tyrone the bright flax grows,
The blackbird sings
And past the farm a quiet river flows.

MARY DEVENPORT O'NEILL (1879 – 1967)

Born Loughrea, Co. Galway, daughter of a police constable. Educated at Eccles Street College and the National College of Art, Dublin. In 1908 married the poet Joseph O'Neill. Mary's first interest was combining ballet with acting and verse-speaking in the performance of verse plays. She also kept a 'salon' at their Rathgar home and became consultant to W.B. Yeats while he wrote *A Vision*. She composed lyrics for her husband's verse play *The Kingdom-Maker*. Her one-act plays *Bluebeard* and *Cain* were produced by Austin Clarke's lyric theatre company in 1933 and 1945. Her long poem 'Prometheus' is in five parts. She explains: '. . . in its most external and most continuous symbolism is an effort to follow the labours and struggles of the creative artist'. Prometheus sees the things that are, the Storyteller (who represents the imagination of Prometheus) sees the things that may be. This poem deserves reprinting.

Her only published volume is *Prometheus and other poems*, London: Jonathan Cape, 1929, from which the poetry here has been selected.

AN OLD WATERFORD WOMAN

On the road over head,
To the passers-by,
'Listen,' she said,
'Inside this cliff are the dead.
They cry
Because they are dead.'
'You hear,' said I,
'The cry
Of the wind in the hollow face of the cliff:
Within the cliff
There is only earth.'

94

'And what,' she said,
'Are the dead
But earth?'

WISHES

I'll take
The shallow loops the blackbirds make
In their low flight,
And gather the strange white
That changes a green field as night comes on;
I'll catch the bars of light,
Before they're gone,
That blinking eyes bring down from the moon,
And make my wishes out of these,
That if I please
I can dissolve them soon —
In time to save them from reality;
The toughness of its stuff would trouble me.

PRAISE

Once with praising I was as tense
As a salmon must be at the salmon leap.
I was wound up to sweep
The world and sky and all experience,
And gather up some new extravagance.
Then, like a flash, I knew that all I'd tried
Was worse than nothing; that being stupified,
Oppressed, impressed, pressed under,
Blurred like the worm,
Dumb beneath a load of wonder,
At last was praise;
And staring on the ground
I sat limp-handed — swung full circle round.

BLANAID SALKELD (1880 – 1959)

Born Chittagong (Pakistan), of Irish parents. Her father was
in the Indian medical service. Her childhood was spent mainly
in Ireland. She married an English member of the Indian Civil
Service, living with him in Bombay and Dacca. She then
returned to Ireland and joined the second company of the
Abbey Theatre, as Nell Byrne. Only one of her unpublished
verse plays was performed, *Scarecrow over the Corn*, at the
Gate in the 1930s. She also translated Pushkin's poems into
English.

Her first volume of verse '... *the engine is left running'*, Dublin: Gayfield Press, 1937, was illustrated by her son Cecil ffrench Salkeld. 'Returning' and 'On the Rand (on Dit)' come from this collection. A second slim volume was *Experiment in Error*, Aldington, Kent: The Hand and Flower Press, 1955, from which comes 'Mostly Supersonic'. She also wrote two books of poems, *Hello Eternity* (1933) and *A Dubliner* (1942). This is a gifted woman, whose poetry reflects her quirkish individualism, and I do not concur with Hogan's criticism of it. Her granddaughter, Beatrice, married Brendan Behan, so Mrs Salkeld also appears in *My Life with Brendan*.

RETURNING

At the crossroads I came upon the delinquent moon,
Uttering brightness, even as an endless word —
Flooding all sound beside. If nestling stirred,
You could not know: all noises overstrewn
By the illimitable bright speech of the moon.
It seems, all matter into spirit blossoms
Where the hushed night birds lave their dusky bosoms
In that broad river slipping from the moon.
Look back. Over the wall, shadows of trees
Appear more dense than their realities ...
The mealy mountains, stirless as a swoon,
Pulse to the slow, sweet slipping from the unlidded moon.

ON THE RAND (*on Dit*)

Can it be verity? ...
While owners put on too much flesh,
Inadequate the miners' dish.
Yet, when the cease-work siren hoots,
These have to scrape mud off their boots
For overseers to set in sieves
The particles of gold it gives.
They clean and weigh, and, locked, despatch —
With penetrating guards to watch —
(Hunger's shade grumbles from a ditch)
In order to enrich the rich.

MOSTLY SUPERSONIC

Man's jungle howl is mostly supersonic —
Else many moderns would — long civilized
Into cold crooked sinning — start, surprised
Out of their sleek beds, at a dim mnemonic

Inner response. The interval is tonic.
But primal echoes, in the most advised
Puppets, cling on, unguessed, unrecognised.
Reaction, yes — but toneless and laconic.
Joy comes of strife; the quiet are not gay.
Only an odd man, though the fashions flout him —
Sensing the grandeur of his hermit soul —
Laughs to recall the muffled jungle howl,
And walks abroad, and shakes the clouds about him —
To lose himself in patterns of the day.

WINIFRED M. LETTS (1882 — c.1950)

Educated at St Anne's Abbots, Bromley and Alexandra College, Dublin, her grandfather was Alexander Ferriro, of Knockmaroon Park, Co. Dublin. Her parents lived in Blackrock. Letts became a masseuse, and later married W.H.F. Verschoyle, living latterly in Kent, where she died. She wrote two one-act plays for the Abbey, *The Eyes of the Blind* (1907), and *The Challenge* (1909), and a three-act play, *Hamilton and Jones* (1941) for the Gate Theatre. She also wrote short stories for children, hagiography and reminiscences, *Knockmaroon* (1933).

Her *Songs from Leinster*, Dundalk: Dundalgan Press, 1947, from which 'Down the boreen' and 'Prayer for a little child' are taken, is a selection of verse from two earlier volumes, *Songs from Leinster*, London 1913, reprinted six times until 1928, and *More Songs from Leinster*, London & New York 1926. 'If love of mine' comes from *Hallow-e'en and poems of the war*, London: Smith Elder, 1916.

IF LOVE OF MINE

If love of mine could witch you back to earth
It would be when the bat is on the wing,
The lawn dew-drenched, the first stars glimmering,
The moon a golden slip of seven nights' birth.
If prayer of mine could bring you it would be
To this wraith-flowered jasmine-scented place
Where shadow trees their branches interlace;
Phantoms we'd tread a land of fantasy.
If love could hold you I would bid you wait
Till the pearl sky is indigo and till
The plough show silver lamps beyond the hill
And Aldebaran burns above the gate.
If love of mine could lure you back to me
From the rose gardens of eternity.

DOWN THE BOREEN

If you let Sorrow in on you,
Surely she'll stay,
Sitting there by the hearth
Till you wish her away.

If you see the grey cloak of her
Down the boreen,
Let you close the door softly
And wait there unseen.

For if she comes in on you
Never you'll part,
Till the fire burns out
In the core of your heart.

PRAYER FOR A LITTLE CHILD

God keep my jewel this day from danger;
From tinker and pooka and black-hearted stranger.
From harm of the water, from hurt of the fire.
From the horns of the cows going home to the byre.
From the sight of the fairies that maybe might change her.
From teasing the ass when he's tied to the manger.
From stones that would bruise her, from thorns of the briar.
From red evil berries that wake her desire.
From hunting the gander and vexing the goat.
From the depths o' sea water by Danny's old boat.
From cut and from tumble, from sickness and weeping;
May God have my jewel this day in his keeping.

TEMPLE LANE (1899 – 1982)

Real name Mary Isabel Leslie, born Dublin, but spent child-
hood in Tipperary. Educated in England and at Trinity College,
Dublin, where she won the Large Gold Medal (1922), and later
became a doctor of philosophy. See Mary Rose Callaghan's sar-
castic entry in Hogan's *Dictionary*, in which Lane's numerous
novels are condemned as 'female fiction before the liberation',
and her verses 'little more than skillful rhyming and merry
tinkles'. The reader must here judge for himself.

Lane also wrote under the name of 'Jean Herbert'. Her
poetry was published in *Dublin Magazine, Dublin Opinion,
The Irish Times, Country Life, The Sunday Independent,
Irish Writing*, etc.

'The Emigrant' comes from *Curlews*, Dublin: The Talbot Press, 1946. 'O'Driscoll's Courting' is from *Fisherman's Wake*, London: Longmans, 1940. Her poem 'The Fairy Tree', set to music by Vincent O'Brien, became very popular.

THE EMIGRANT

He goes to the furrows
Where no crops are found:
He goes to the wild field —
The field without bound.

He goes to the tillage
That swallows a plough,
And the shapes of my terror
Sink after him now:

And now up to Heaven
My bright prayers are sped.
Till the stars that were falling
Are rising instead —

Till the danger-strewn waters
Are firm for his ease
As the flagstones of churches
We mark with our knees.

O'DRISCOLL'S COURTING

She said — 'You saw me in a child's white dress,
    With wreath and veil my First Communion day,
A little bride — and do this wickedness?
    What would that holy man the Bishop say?'
    I laughed — 'He's buried!' and she sobbed — 'I'll pray!'

Below the cliffs the sea comes thieving in,
    (The room she had looked out upon the sea!)
Stroking on sand smooth as a woman's skin:
    And no one watched that night but her and me,
    And maybe monks above in Mellary.

'O'Driscoll!' chaps would whisper. 'There's the lad!
    Oh, that's the devil has the women tame!
But still-an'-all . . . send that-one to the bad?
    Not even he would try that wicked shame,
    God help us!' And she loved my very name.

But marry? Is it marry? Be dragged down
    Each year with brats and drink, like some you meet?
I knew a dozen girls beyond in town
    Would give me all I wanted, give it sweet,
    And none of them was fit to dust her feet.

So quiet all that early night she prayed,
    While my great wish was powerful strong to fight
That far, against her prayer: and there I stayed
    Out in the haggart, watching for a light,
    Knowing her father would sleep deaf and tight.

Against her prayer, my will: as strong to crush
    As carrion crow upon a lamb's weak head:
Picking its eyes out, thrashing it to slush.
    Against her faith, her love: against her dread
    Greater I'll be than all the Saints, I said.

Stronger than God I'll be, if so with Him
    She thinks They'll bring great influence to bear,
As I would go to Rooney and say — 'Tim,
    You've influence: now, use it for me there!' —
    'Tis much the same I understand with prayer.

And so I stayed: until I saw a light
    Shake in the room, and watched her fully dressed
Kneel at the window taller than her height,
    With lifted chin and hands upon her breast,
    Praying against me as against the pest.

(I'd said — 'It's not my voice will bring you, not
    My throat, but my great wish, will make the call.
You wouldn't leave me in the ditch to rot
    Like any spud from cart or pit let fall —
    Come out to me, come out and bring your shawl!'

I knew she'd come when I had made her cry,
    Reddening the sweetest eyes God ever lit,
Twisting her mouth to make it tell a lie.
    And so I coaxed her — 'Scared of me a bit?'
    'Oh, not of you, but sin! — afraid of it!')

One minute she was in the window square:
    And then the light went dark, and she came through.
Oh, I was rich with pride that she would dare!
    And my desire came living, and came new.
    And — 'Girl,' I said, 'myself is here for you!'

I saw her widened eyes, and then a whiff
    Of shaking air divided, so that she
Walked past me (right, or left?) across the cliff

Like a crane's flight, and vanished to the sea —
My mind had had her, but her soul was free.

Perhaps I yelled: and if at the cliff head
  I didn't pitch myself where she had gone
'Twas that I hoped she maybe wasn't dead,
  Caught on a rock-shelf. With the moon full on
There wasn't beast or Christian where it shone.

Perhaps I prayed, while like a goat I crawled
  Down to the fingering sea to bring her back.
The tide possessed the sand: the foam was scrawled
  Like slavered spittle where the weed lay black —
I searched for her in every pile of wrack.

And did I find her? 'Twasn't I that found
  My white dead love at morning, by the powers!
Within her window, lying on the ground,
  The life that lit her prayed away for hours.
They waked her there with candles and with flowers.

I, eighty years, tell any lad to-day,
  When Faith has left you for your lust, have sense!
If you should harm a girl who starts to pray
  You'll never make your soul for pounds or pence —
  Virgins in Heaven control great influence.

RHODA SINCLAIR COGHILL (1903 –)

Born Dublin. Educated at Alexandra College, then studied at
Read Pianoforte School and became a professor there after
qualifying. LRAM and ARCM, also holds B Music degree from
University College, Dublin. Later became pupil of Artur
Schnabel in Berlin. Official Accompanist of Radio Eireann
from 1939, also a concert pianist, and has made recordings
for Radio Eireann. She translated Rilke, and took to writing
poetry after an illness. Her verse was published in *The Dublin
Magazine, The Irish Times, Irish Press* and *The Bell.* She since
published two volumes of poetry. 'In the City' is from *The
Bright Hillside*, Dublin: Hodges, Figgis, 1948, 'Flight' from
Time is a squirrel, published for the author at Dolmen Press,
1956.

FLIGHT

This is the road that since the summer — since
their parting — she shunned, for fear of meeting him.

Until the time of ripening their quarrel
lasted, and in September, when the harvest
was brimming in the fields, she went her way
by other paths. Through any opening gate
he suddenly might come, on a waggon loaded
with tousled grain; and when mists of a mild October
crawled on the sodden soil, he would be cutting
his straggled hedges, time-serving till the sullen
fallow land should harden with more than the first
gossamer frost, and open to winter work.
But today she takes that road in the late afternoon
when already across the bloodshot sky the rooks
are blinking home. She is no longer afraid while
the year lasts, knowing the watchdog daylight
whines in November on a shortened leash.
She holds her scarf tightened along her cheek;
her worn shoes make no noise but a crisp soft
crushing of frozen grass and ivy and dock,
that keep her footsteps, still as a pattern in damask.
She moves in the ditch of the drab lane, patched with agate
ice-pools, dried after sharp showers by a long
sweeping wind. Her ears tell that beyond
the sheltering hedge two horses — a stubble-dappled
roan, and a mare as red as springing sally
whips or a burnt-out beech — are treading the dead-branch
crumbling clay, that breaks against the metal
harrow's teeth . . . He shouts to make them turn;
behind him turns a cloud of white sea-birds . . .

She keeps to the near ditch; but the road winding
and bending again shows a new-made breach in the briars.
At the treacherous gap she stops. Oh! now to run,
to hide like a feathered frightened thing in the dusk!
But she who thought to pass like a bird or a bat,
encountering only the hedge-high gulls, is trapped:
for the too-familiar face, the known shape
walking the furrows, are seen . . . So it was vain
to shield evasive eyes, to discipline
rebellious feet: vain to her and to him
the fugitive pretence. For a proud pulse
beats in her brain like a startled wing; the blood
tramples its path in the stubborn heart's field
with the eightfold stamping hooves of a strong team
of horses; and she feels, raking the flesh,
the harrow of love's remembered violence.

IN THE CITY

Gently in the night flows my river, the Liffey.
It is mine by right of love, this river always
Running, since childhood, under my feet, always

102

Branching along my veins — this river of birds,
Avenue of serene, Ascendancy swans,
Trail of the single gunman cormorant,
Stage of the seagulls' ballet — those faery visitors
Who cry and perch and fly, blown in the air
Like paper toys.
                         Tonight there are no birds;
The thickening mist blinds me to all but light.
By day small painted boats, wings
Of coloured parrots, tighten their holding ropes
And lie beside the wall. Pale women
Hurry across the bridges, dawdle at windows,
Treasure their handbags, intent on finding bargains.
Crowds at the rush-hour of a Spring afternoon
Move in the clean patterns of thrown confetti.
                                          But now
In fog the city covers all its candour.
From windowed vehicles the light
Imprints a moving tartan on the water;
And where a street-lamp hangs a luminous triangle,
There, mirrored, a three-sided corresponding
Euclidean figure breaks the river's blackness,
Base to base applied, with lamp-post perpendicular
And tree subtending.
                              Now
Where are the seabirds? Do they fly
At day's end to the sea, to spend the night
One-legged on rock, in thought?
When, rarely, moves a patch
Of faint illumination on the darkest water,
Then are discovered small waiting forms,
Patiently floating, homeless, through the dark
They do not understand. Silence
Holds them, until daylight.

LORNA REYNOLDS (1911 –)

Born Kingston, Jamaica, of Irish parents, and became a leading academic in Ireland. Attached to the English department of University College, Dublin, 1940-66, then Professor of Modern English, University College, Galway 1966-78. Editor of *University Review* 1954-66, and of *Yeats Studies* (with Robert O'Driscoll) 1970-77. She has published verse and critical studies in Ireland, England and on the Continent, but her poetry remains uncollected. Her latest work is: *Kate O'Brien: a literary portrait*, Gerrards Cross: Colin Smythe, 1986.

'Euridyce' was published in *Arena*, No. 1, Spring, 1963.

Ah, the shining castle over the water
That rose to my sight,
Softly bright,
As you me, apostate from deity,
Exile from the orb of light,
Led back from the long occlusion of the night,
You Orpheus, me Euridyce.

My heavy hand travelled along the rainbow
And dabbled in marble sparks;
At the end of my lashes
Suns hung swinging on every blink;
My fingers glowed ruby-red, as me,
Up the long tunnel from night to day, you led,
You Orpheus, me Euridyce.

Your flute split petals beneath my feet;
In links of flowers I stepped.
Cowslip-sweet the breath
Blown down the dazzling southern-facing shaft,
As we climbed and wound from dusty underground,
Up far on the way, you leading me,
You Orpheus, me Euridyce.

O, Orpheus, farewell; for now we part.
I turn at the mouth
Of the way,
And you me, apostate from deity,
Exile from the orb of light,
Send back to the long occlusion of the night,
Oh, Orpheus! your lost Euridyce.

MARY LAVIN (1912 –)

Born East Walpole, Massachusetts, of recently emigrated Irish
parents who returned to Athenry in 1921, then moved first
to Dublin, then to Co. Meath. Educated Loreto Convent, and
University College, Dublin (1st Hons. English). Taught French
at the Loreto Convent. Started to write in the midst of a
Ph.D. thesis on Virginia Woolf, which was never completed.
Married a Dublin lawyer William Walsh (1942) and moved to
a farm at Bective, Co. Meath. Her husband died in 1954 leaving
her, already established as a writer, with three daughters.
She re-married M. MacDonald Scott (1969) and at present
divides her time between Bective and a Dublin apartment.

She was elected President of the Irish Academy of Letters 1972/3 and is a recipient of the Aosdana. Besides two Guggenheim Fellowships Lavin has won many prizes for her short stories, such as the Katherine Mansfield Award and the Ella Lynam Cabot Award, and her reputation as one of Ireland's leading short story writers is now assured. She has also written two novels, but little poetry. Her work has been published widely in Ireland, the United States, and Britain, etc., translated into several languages, and adapted for radio and television. Her stories have been collected in three volumes by Constable (London) and Houghton Mifflin (Boston). There is also a more recent Penguin selection (London 1981, New York 1984), and *A Family Likeness*, Constable, 1985. My own study of her short stories, *Mary Lavin: Quiet Rebel*, Dublin: Wolfhound Press, 1980, contains a bibliography which already needs updating.

Her untitled poem chosen here was printed in *Dublin Magazine* 15, Jan./Mar. 1940.

CHRIST IF YOU WANTED MY SHINING SOUL

Christ if you wanted my shining soul
That flashed its happy fins
And splashed in the silent seas of sin,
Then Christ, keenest fisherman
on the Galilean shore,
If you wanted to catch my shivering soul
Why did you let down nets that were worn,
Unravelled and floating light?
I slid along the ribbony web
In and out
And when the nets slime-wet and black
Crawled over the prow of your boat again
Empty as nets that sway all day
In an empty sea
My sly soul waited
And swam aloft
To play at leaping the ripples
And showing its silver dapples
To the silently floating fishes
On the outer-side of the wave
The little silver minnows of the moon.

MADGE HERRON (c.1917 –)

Born near Fintown, Co. Donegal of a very poor peasant family, and worked first as a Gaelic-speaking nurse or 'skivvy'. Studied at the School of Acting, Abbey Street, Dublin, and obtained a scholarship to the Royal Academy of Dramatic Art, London. Wrote 'Rory O'Donnell' staged (1939) at Croydon Repertory theatre. Has written other one-act plays and read these and stories on Radio Eireann and the BBC, especially the girl's part opposite Frank O'Connor in 'The Midnight Court' (1948). She has also done readings at the Abbey and Peacock theatres, Dublin. She studied English at evening classes, and is therefore largely a self-educated poet. Madge says: 'I am very politically oriented and want to give my poems back to the county that bred me'. Her poems, she says, are 'millions of years old', and do not belong to her. She now lives in London. Poetry chosen here was originally published in 'The Rat Pit', *Donegal Democrat*, the editor of which paper, Gerard Moriarty, interviewed Herron in September 1980. Her work deserves wider recognition.

A POEM FOR FRANCIS HARVEY

Christ, and when I sleep
Your wounds hop on to me
like little mice:
what encumbrance is this?
Survive the night
and be my finest poem
pushed thinly through
and nothing of you spilt.
A legend in a vessel;
twixt the gable
and the well
whortled darkening stones
near where you fell
I hear Him coming
in the mass.
Will He love me?
who am the Bull –
and will He say?
There's not a day
goes past
But I think on thee,
My Love, My Love.

Listening to that blackguard
heap abuse upon the bonhams
has me drenched.
If He can see fit
to making a row the
like of that —
and they but a few days old,
what will happen
the day He sticks them?
From now on
it's plush velvet for me
I refuse to settle for anything less.
I put it to him
and his reply to me was?
I could go and kiss his arse
but what brings you?
on this of all days,
Good Friday!
the ceiling low,
the house surrounded by soldiers,
and me entirely convinced
I am the mother of one,
I forget his name right now,
all morning.
I've been sending myself up,
I'm a great one for make-believe,
I was put out of heaven for it.
They said, you lack initiative
go and fetch us a million
Green Shield stamps
and we will give you
another chance.
It was a tremendous challenge.
When you are eighteen
you feel you can go anywhere.
At the same time,
you can go bloody no place.
I tallyho'd back on to earth
one Christmas Eve
coming in low
over the Urals.
That great slug of a beast
Yeats saw tiptoeing towards Bethlehem,
that was me.
Have you ever been to Russia
Mr. Pound?
In the Urals
there are these draught corridors,
they go in and out like melodeons,

the music they make
has a static effect on
the winds above.
You don't get buffeted
neither are you sucked in.
I was thinking Mr. Pound:
a couple of hundred years from now
you will be a forest
night bellowing the bat to prayer.
Ever since I read
you had gone
and turned yourself into a tree
I had a feeling I ought
to go and stand next to you.
I was on my way to you with a looking glass
when the weather broke
and I had to turn back.
How come? 'Tis Sappho
who loved Atthis long ago
rocks your child to sleep?
That one never had a head for heights!
Call to her to come down
before she hurts herself.
Once, she was my neighbour,
she owned a black pig.
Oh! many a Sunday after mass,
I have stood and watched them copulate.
The immensity
of what has happened to you,
has you subdued.
The lullaby is all gone out of you.
What? No little song for me?
(little brown elf —
a song, a song?)
Go crack the bell black
dome of night!
Slip through and grab the moon,
furl her out.
Be quick about it.
Last time they threatened you
it was in Islamic,
now it's the man
with the see-through mint.
Get up in the rafters
and hide yourself,
while I go and open the door.
It would never do
if one of them
was to take you
for an IRA man.
I have no way

of proving
you really are
Ezra Pound!

MÁIRE MHAC AN tSAOI (1922 –)

Born Dublin, daughter of Seán Mac Entee, one-time Sinn
Féin member for Monaghan, who became deputy prime
minister under Mr de Valera. Educated University College,
Dublin, Dublin Institute for Advanced Studies and at the
Sorbonne; called to the Irish Bar and joined the Department
of External Affairs, serving in Paris and Madrid. Worked on
the preparation of the standard English/Irish dictionary. She
is now married to Conor Cruise O'Brien, and they have two
adopted children. She cooperated with her husband in *A
Concise History of Ireland*, London: Thames & Hudson,
1972. Her published poetry includes: *Margadh na Saoire*,
Dublin 1956; *A Heart Full of Thought* (translations from the
Irish), Dublin 1959; *Codladh an Ghaiscígh*, Dublin 1973 (title
poem chosen from this volume); *An Galar Dubhach*, Dublin
1980, from which 'Fomhar na Farraige' comes; *An Cion Go
Dtí Seo*, Sairséal Ó Marcaigh, Dublin 1987.

CODLADH AN GHAISCÍGH

Ceannín mogallach milis mar sméar –
A mhaicín iasachta, a chuid den tsaoil,
Dé do bheathasa is neadaigh im chróí,
Dé do bheathasa fé fhrathacha an tí,
A réilthín maidine 'tháinig i gcéin.

Is maith folaíocht isteach!
Féach mo bhullán beag d'fhear;
Sáraigh sa doras é nó ceap
I dtubán – Chomh folláin le breac
Gabhaimse orm! Is gach ball fé rath,
An áilleacht mar bharr ar an neart –

109

Do thugais ón bhfómhar do dhath
Is ón rós crón. Is deas
Gach buí óna chóngas leat.
Féach, a Chonchúir, ár mac,
Ní mar beartaíodh ach mar cheap
Na cumhachta in airde é 'theacht.

Tair go dtím' bachlainn, a chircín eornan,
Tá an lampa ar lasadh is an oíche ag tórmach,
Tá an mada rua ag siúl an bóthar,
Nár sheola aon chat mara ag snapadh é id threosa,
Nuair gur tú coinneal an teaghlaigh ar choinnleoirín óir duit.

Id shuan duit fém' borlach
Is fál umat mo ghean —
Ar do chamachuaird má sea
Fuar agam bheith dhed' bhrath.
Cén chosaint a bhéarfair leat?
Artha? Leabharúin? Nó geas?
'Ná taobhaigh choíche an geal,'
Paidir do chine le ceart.

Ar nós gach máthar seal
Deinim mo mhachnamh thart
Is le linn an mheabhraithe
Siúd spíonóig mhaide id ghlaic!
Taibhrítear dom go pras
An luan láich os do chneas
I leith is gur chugham a bheadh,
Garsúinín Eamhna, Cú na gCleas!

THE HERO'S SLEEP

Little clustered head sweet as the blackberry,
Little foreign son, my part of this world,
Welcome and nest in my heart,
Welcome under the rafters of this house,
Little morning star come from a long way off.

Blood from without is good;
Look at my little bull calf of a man;
Head him off from the doorway
Or wedge him in a tub:
As healthy as a trout, I swear it!
And every limb prospering:
Beauty a crown for strength —

You took your colour from the autumn
And from the dun rose;
Every yellow is beautiful from its relationship with you.
See Conor our son
Not as was planned, but as
The higher powers willed his coming

Come to my arms, little barley hen,
The lamp is lighting and the night is threatening;
The fox is walking the road;
May no cat from the sea lead him snapping in your direction,
Since you are the candle of the household on a little golden
                                         candlestick.
When you are asleep under my breast
My love is a wall about you —
But when you set out on your kingly progress
It is in vain for me to spy on you:
What defence will you bring with you?
A charm? A talisman? Or a taboo?
'Never trust the white',
Is the proper prayer for your race.

Like every mother at times
I turn over thoughts in my mind,
And while I dwell on them,
Suddenly you have caught up a wooden spoon!
On the instant as in a dream I see
The hero's light over your countenance,
As though coming towards me there were
The little boy from Eamhain, the Hound of Feats!

(Author's translation)

FOMHAR NA FARRAIGE

Sheo linn ar thórramh an Gharlaigh Choileánaigh
Is i ndoras an tseomra bhí romhainn an mháithrín,
'A mhaicín ó,' ar sí, 'Ní raibh críne i ndán duit
Is is dual don óige bheith fiain rascánta —
Is ochón!' ...

Fíoghar ar mo shúile iad cneácha míofara a mic,
Is snagaíl fhiata a ghlórtha is teinn trém chluasaibh —
An gearrcach gránna an dá uair báite againn,
Greas insa tsrúill is greas fén mbladar tomtha —
Is ochón!

Lasann 'na ghnúis chugham an dá shméaróid dhóite;
Rian na gcúig mhéar mo leiceadarsa 'tharraing
Tráth gabhadh é is a ladhar aige sa phróca ...
Is duitse atáim á insint, a phoill an fhalla!
Is ochón!

'gCloistí an mháthair? 'Fé mar chaith sé liomsa!
Is tar éis gur fhág príosún d'fhill ar an bhfaoistin' ...
Do scar an mhrúch a folt glas-uaithne ar Chonaing —
D'fhuadaigh ó fhód na croiche an cincíseach!
Is ochón!

Amhantarán ón gceallúraigh in' aithbhreith
Ag sianaíl choíche ar rian na daonnachta!
Iarlais ins a' tsíog gaoithe ar neamhmbeith!
Coillteán na trua ón aithis dhéanach so!
Is ochón!

Ná bí ag brath ormsa, 'ainniseoir!
Id cháilíocht fhéin dob ann duit dá shuaraí í —
Ach ní réitíonn an marbh is an beo
Hook your own ground! Ní mise bard do chaointe —
Is ochón! . . .

Éignigh a ghreim den ngunail — bíodh acu!
Cuir suas an t-íomhá céireach i measc na gcoinneall
An féinics gléasta tar éis a thonachtha,
Is téadh an giobal scéite síos go grinneal —
Is ochón! . . .

Scéal uaim ar thórramh an Gharlaigh Choileánaig
Níor facathas fós dúinn aon tsochraid chomh breá léi,
Cliar agus tuath is an dubh ina bhán ann —
Is bearna a'mhíl i bhfolach fén gclár ann!
Is ochón!

THE HARVEST OF THE SEA

We set off to the wake of the whelpish youngster,
And in the door of the room there before us was the Mammy;
'Oh little son,' said she, 'Old age was not to be your portion,
And it is the part of youth to be wild and rakish —
And ochone!' . . .

Imprinted on my eyes are the unattractive features of her son,
And the eldritch stammer of his voice is a pain through my ears —
We have drowned the ugly chick twice over,
Once in the surge and once submerged in flattery —
And ochone! . . .

Two burnt embers glow at me from his face,
That track of five fingers was left by the slap I gave him
When they caught him with his fist fast in the crock . . .
It is to you I tell it, o hole in the wall!
And ochone! . . .

List to the mother, 'How good he was to me!
And after he came out of jail he returned to the practise of confession' . . .
The sea-wife has spread her blue-green hair over Conaing —
Has snatched the Whitsuntide child from the site of the gallows!
And ochone!' . . .

An abortion, from the graveyard of the unbaptized, reborn
Whining forever after humanity!
A changeling in the shee-wind of unbeing!
Pitiable eunuch after this last outrage!
And ochone!

Put not your trust in me, poor wretch!
However base your quality, at least as such you existed —
But the dead do not suit with the living:
Hook your own ground! I am no bard to keen you —
And ochone! . . .

Force his grip from the gunwale — they have won!
Put up the waxen image among the candles, the Phoenix arrayed after
   his deathwashing,
And let the sloughed rag sink to the sea-bed —
And ochone! . . .

Let me tell you about the wake of the whelpish youngster,
We never saw yet any funeral as splendid,
Clergy and laity and black become white there —
And the hare-lip was hidden beneath the coffin lid!
And ochone!

(Author's translation)

EITHNE STRONG (1923 –)

Born Glensharrold, Co. Limerick, née O'Connell, educated
Carrickerry National School, where both her parents taught,
and at Scoil Mhuire, Ennis. Joined the Civil Service, then
married the poet and psychoanalyst Rupert Strong (d. 1984),
by whom she had nine children. Took a modern languages
degree at Trinity College, Dublin, when in her forties, and
started freelance journalism and book reviewing. She has also
worked as a theatre critic. Eithne now teaches Irish, English
and French, as well as writing short stories and poetry in Irish
and English, and broadcasting. Her work has been widely pub-
lished in periodicals such as *The Dublin Magazine, New Irish
Writing, Orbis, Comhar, The Irish Press, Poetry Ireland,
Hibernia, Aquarius, Broadsheet*, etc. Her publications include:
Songs of Living, Dublin: Runa Press, 1961; *Sarah in Passing*,
Portlaoise: Dolmen Press, 1974; *Degrees of Kindred*, Dublin:
Tansy Books, 1979 (novel); *Flesh . . . the Greatest Sin*, Dublin:
Runa Press, 1980; *Cirt Oibre*, Dublin: Coiscéim; *Patterns*,
Dublin:Poolbeg Press, 1981 (short stories); *Fuil Agus Fallaí*,
Dublin: Coiscéim, 1983;*My darling neighbour*, Dublin: Beaver
Row Press, 1985. 'Ceart Urraime', published in *Hibernia* (in
English), is from her latest Irish collection. 'Dance to your
Daddy' was published in *Portland Review Anthology* (Oregon),
and in *Broadsheet* (Edinburgh), 1983.

CEART URRAIME

A phráta a scamhaim,
cuirtear i bhfeidhm orm
tarraingt uait, amh,
fiú i ngan fhios nach mór,
gan í bheith maol ná garbh
mar a cheapfaí maidir le rud
eascartha ón ísealscraith;
ar shlí aisteach
cuireann tú go réidh i láthair
do cheart urraime, tusa
atá fiarshúileach, crón,
gur taca mo chlainne thú;
braithim i réim
scaoilscéim éigin
a nascann le chéile
mé féin agus tú
tusa óna mbainim craiceann
fad a shuíonn
An Taoiseach i gcomhairle.

NECESSITY FOR REVERENCE

O potato that I peel
I am made to know
your raw appeal
insidious, oddly,
not blunt nor coarse
as might one
expect from something so
crudely sprung;
in some peculiar fashion
you quietly present
your claim for reverence,
you, cockeyed, swarth,
supporter of my family;
I feel a vague design
holds me in curious link
with you whose peel
I strip while the Taoiseach
sits in council

(Author's translation)

from FLESH . . . THE GREATEST SIN

What progeny could issue from such convoluted beginnings?
Inside the womb of Ellen sperm met egg.
A long poison, still virulently strong
from the past of flayings, witches, burnings,
went into that fusion.

The helpless embryo passively received its legacy
of fear, intersticed through the cankered being. (What does
fear do to flesh that should be spirit's blossoming?)
The old Voices of Authority always ruled in Ellen;
oddly, they did not condemn pride of place
but declared to be Hell pride in flesh:
her daughter, Nance, must from the first be cauterised.

To prevent sin
this girl must be
made to see herself ugly.
Ah, your shape
'tis pitiful,
lank, thin,
nothing to be proud of;
and isn't it you that brought
the sallow skin:
dead spit of your cracked aunt,
Mary Kate — God rest her . . .

but sure 'tis a blessing
to be ugly:
you're better off
than to be
always preening —
that leads to mortal sin.

Flesh, the corruptible mould that grows on bones,
the particularly dangerous outgrowth on chest,
ingrowth between legs — that unthinkable lurk
impossible to purify — must, because
of intrinsic sulliedness, be purged incessantly.

DANCE TO YOUR DADDY

He had his way with her when she was fourteen.
Some would say there should have been abortion;
to that the parents should have seen.

They did not and I am here. Of course there was
a marriage. The parents did see to that.
My mother was fifteen when I was born.

They had a room, one the parents gave them.
For her sake. He never got up in the mornings.
Everyone says I cried a lot. I can

remember screaming, fighting. He hit her.
They tangled on the floor where I was.
I saw everything. They did it all

115

in front of me. Soon I had a brother. They were
in two rooms then. Her parents gave rent. But he
never got up. Five o'clock in the evening that was

his time. When he left us my mother shook and shook.
She was very thin. Once
he took my brother and me to a place

where a girl was always with him. They did
everything before us. I copied them.
I went up on my brother. They laughed.

But he never got up in the mornings. The girl
paid for things. She always had money. She
stuffed soap in my mouth when I cursed.

I cursed the curses he did. After a while
he took us back again to my mother. Men were
often with her. None of them

ever got up in the mornings. Men always
slept. When they finished sleeping
other men came. One man stayed longer

than the others. But not until night
did he get up. Sometimes my mother
took us to school. Now I am a man.

I sleep a lot and take welfare benefit.

LELAND BARDWELL (1928 –)

Née Hone, born India, of Irish parents. Grew up in Leixlip,
educated in Dublin. Has also lived in Paris and London. She
now lives in Dublin, and has three sons. She began writing
poetry aged seven. She is co-editor of *Cyphers* (Dublin). Her
literary output has been as follows: Radio plays for the BBC
and RTE, other drama includes 'Thursday', produced at
Trinity College in 1972; 'Open-ended Prescription', at the
Peacock, Dublin (1979); 'No Regrets' (about Edith Piaf), at
the Gorey Arts Festival (1983). Her collections of poems are:
The Mad Cyclist, Dublin: New Writers, 1970; *The Fly and the
Bedbug*, Dublin: Beaver Row Press, 1984. Her reputation as a
novelist is growing, see *Girl on a bicycle*, Dublin: Coop Books,
1977; *That London Winter*, Dublin: Coop Books, 1981; *The
House*, Dingle: Brandon, 1984; *Different Kinds of Love*
(stories), Dublin: Attic Press, 1987. 'The Scattering of Ashes'
was published in *Cyphers* 15, 1981.

116

THE SCATTERING OF THE ASHES

The grass that's flattened by the orchestra of wind
lies polished for the tenderness of hand,
the stroking of this well-trod shoulder,
not green but yellow and anything but pleasant.
Named Downs they lift to the lined horizon,
shrug off the factory town below;
like grey uncarded hair,
smoke straggles from the pear-shaped chimneys.

And there are seven, connected
by blood or breath, with bowed heads
& gammon cheeks, who falter unevenly in the dried-out ruts
as brother holds brother in a cardboard box.
Confused in his own flesh he offers it windward
his fingers ringed by the twine —
It's barely big enough to parcel
an inexpensive clock.
Of what do they chat or whom do they discover
in the this and that of ceremony?

Pulverised bone is grey and carbon to the touch,
adheres to palms and the edges of the nails.
As each shakes forth his individual veil,
the wind gusts and divides the matrices;
the immediate matter is settled with the dust
that curious beasts have recently disturbed.

Married, long divorced, a couple
in this funeral of chords
unreels a filament of memory.
It's a safe bargaining with the merchandise of years;
the spit-on-the-hand, the luck-penny that's returned.

EVANGELINE PATERSON (1928 –)

Born Limavady, raised in Dublin. Married a professor of geography, has two sons and a daughter, and lives in Leicester. She is an editor of *Other Poetry* and her work has appeared in *The Irish Press, Envoi, New England Review, Other Poetry* and the *American Yearbook of Magazine Verse, Rialto, Acumen* and *Stand*. Her first two published collections of verse (1972 and 1978) are out of print. Poems chosen here come from the third collection, *Bringing the Water Hyacinth to Africa*, Stamford: Taxus Press, 1983. She has also written *How to Write Your Own Poems* with cartoons by her son, a mini-manual for new poets, published by *Other Poetry*.

WIFE TO HUSBAND

you are a person
like a tree
standing like rock
moving like water

you show me how
to hold like a root
and how to dance
in a changing rhythm

you hold me close
in a singing stillness
you rock me slow
in a crazy wind

you show me a height
that I may grow to
you cover the sky
with stars and branches

you lose your leaves
without complaining
you know there will be
another spring

you stand like rock
you move like water
you are a person
like a tree

ARMAMENTS RACE

and Mrs Stephanopoulos said oh yes I am happy
I am very happy and why not for I have
a fine husband and beautiful children

and we have our health and enough to eat and we all
love each other exceedingly and if I had just one wish
this is what it would be

that when we die we should all go to heaven together
in the same instant so that none might feel
pain or despair at the losing of any other

and I said oh Mrs Stephanopoulos oh my dear
you should be truly a happy woman for never
have so many been toiling with such a blinkered devotion
in the deep-down mines and the shiny laboratories
to make your one wish come true.

BIDDY JENKINSON (1929 –)

Living at present in Glendalough, Co. Wicklow, writes only in Irish. Her work has been published in *Inntí, Poetry Ireland, Comhar, Feasta, Déidre, Riverine*. Her first collection is *Baisteadh Gintlí*, Dublin: Coiscéim, 1987.

CIÚNAS

Fáilte romhat a bhradáin bhig
a chaith an bhroinn le confadh saoil.
Gabhaim orm bheith mar abhainn
dod chúrsa óm chom go sáile i gcéin.

Scaoil do racht is ól go faíoch.
Súigh uaim suan. I gconradh cíche
súfad siar ó lúb do bheoil
gean le tál arís go buíoch.

Fáilte romhat a bhradáin suain
dhein lánlinn chiúnin i sruth mo shaoil.
Ar sheol do chuisle airím ceol
na nUile dom sheoladh féin.

How I welcome you, little salmon/ who leapt the womb, impatient to commence life./ I undertake to be a river to you/ as you follow your course from the haven of my belly to far distant seas./
Let yourself go, and drink up your fill./ Suck sleep from me. By the terms of the breast-contract/ I'll suck back from your puckered lips/ love, with which I'll suckle another time, and/ for that I'm grateful./ How I welcome you, salmon of sleep/ who made a tranquil pool in my life-stream./ In the rhythm of your heartbeat/ I hear the music of the Heavens,/ and it guides my way. *(Translation: Padraigín Riggs)*

MAEVE KELLY (1930 –)

Born and educated Dundalk. Student nurse in London, then nursed in Oxford and Ireland. Lived in Co. Clare and farmed there for many years. Now lives near Limerick with husband and two children.

From 1974 involved in women's movement and now administrates the Limerick Refuge for Battered Wives. She broadcasts on RTE, gives readings and runs writers' workshops in Ireland. *A Life of Her Own* (short stories), Dublin: Poolbeg Press, 1976; *Necessary Treasons* (novel), London: Michael Joseph, 1985, paperbacked (Methuen), 1986; *Resolution* (poetry), Belfast: Blackstaff Press, 1986, from which 'Half Century' is taken. Won 1972 Hennessy Literary Award.

HALF CENTURY

Others have not been lucky as we
Who have shared these generous times,
Welding together even in absence
Every present moment, so that we become
Almost one flesh, each self-sufficient
Though interdependent. Siamese twins.
It would not be true to say there have been
No rows, no flurry of disparate views,
Flaring to rooftop high
Our loud sundering of old vows.
They have been rare and only memorable
Because of that.
Yet our lives have not been placid —
The usual deaths, the common griefs,
The surge and swell of children,
Bad school reports, drugs in a window box,
Even the policeman at the door.

When I look back through my half century
I am astonished to discover
That for only half of it
I have known you. The other half
Collapses on itself by this default.
That first growth seems in retrospect
A kind of vagrancy, a maverick uncertainty
Without anchorage. An unrewarded search.

I am overwhelmed by the dicey chance of this.

Other lovers write in praise
Or in cherished recall of the intimacies
Which, being secret, are shattered by a phrase.
I cannot describe the puzzle we have made,
Jig-sawing miraculously, fitting our variety,
Our patchwork lives, our woven cloth,
Many-textured, many-coloured, into this tent
With which we clothe and house ourselves.

These are the things we have together made,
Gardens and houses, walls I know will stand
Long after we are gone. Vistas have opened
And closed to our command,
And the buttressed land has been breached
And yielded a little. All may remain
When we unfold ourselves in twin plots
And return separately to that dust
Which gave us common sustenance. It is a grief
I dare not ponder, our separate deaths.
Will we, I wonder, for the next half
Of half a century, with unexplored insight

Unwind, unfold, untangle twined-over roots from roots,
Unravel time itself so that we may slide
Placidly back to birth, and finally divide?

All those unsayable words
You, being private, regard as sacred
Will have found their place.
Can these things we have made
Speak of them, our loves, our fears, our griefs?
Or the nonsensical breakfast discussions,
Politics, the day's bombings, the brute maimings,
The tattered fabric of our outer lives?
Is that what we will leave?

Lovers who are permitted
Mirrored glimpses of each other
Forget the privilege and become familiar.
We have somehow escaped such despair,
Are constantly amused by the absurd.
Perhaps we share
A half-witted simpleness
And regard the world
Through the other's innocence.

ANNE LE MARQUAND HARTIGAN (1931 –)

Born Reading, of an Irish mother and a Jersey father, educated
by the Sacred Heart Order in England and at Reading University
(fine arts). She is an award winning batik artist, with
paintings and batiks in many private collections in Ireland and
England. She also won the Listowel Open poetry award in
1978. Anne has lived in Ireland since 1962. Her long poem
'Now is a moveable Feast', with music composed for it by
Eibhlis Farrell, was broadcast by RTE. Her poetry collections
are *Long Tongue* and *Return Single*, Dublin: Beaver Row Press,
1982 and 1986. Her verse has been published in *Hibernia,
The Irish Press, The Irish Times, Cyphers, Poetry Ireland, The
Ulster Tatler*, and in Scotland and Greece. Her controversial
play *Beds* was performed at the Dublin Theatre Festival 1982.

SMALL HOLDING

1

As a winter breath left in the air,
A hairpin caught in the dust of drawers
Or cracks between floorboards, lying
Close to the thatch where sparrows snuggle

121

For comfort, nest for hornet and wasp, as
Owl note afloat on the dark,

This house will have witnessed many a woman
Push and sweat her child out. And watched
A hard man plunge them in. Groan and sleep.
Cattle munched and moaned here, ropes pulled
The young from the socket. Men red to elbow.
Quivering thigh.

Here, there was height above them. Smoke rose
To swill the rafters, clouding timbers,
Weaving out the dream. Then, leaned beams over
To span and floor, lowered the horizon.
These squatmen had no need to bend at door.

All was practical. No time for the luxury
Of feeling. Passion turned under. Dug in
Against the sod. Rugged weather screeched
The land flat, money hard to unearth,
The expected rhythm of death and birth
Unremarkable. Plod made the soul stiff.

There was not time or cash to carve
A delicate detail on doorpost or knob,
The house plain faced, wattle and daubed. The spirit
Could leap with the sparks from the forge,
The massive logs on the hearth, or lifting
The eyes from the soil to the swift cut air.

2

What happened
When you turned the music on?
Before who played?

Rough fiddle, piper, boot
To drum the mud or tiled floor?
You and I we turned the music on,
I came in, on outside closed the door,
Our feet made dance in and on the night
A music that was ours not played before.

That happened
When we turned the music on.
Who played before?

(Norfolk 1980)

122

ADVENT

Now I will make fat puddings
In the winter evenings,
Huddle home early,
Twist by the fire,
Shutting the door on the dimlight.

It is the going down time.
Curtains pull early
And I am introverted,
There are bogymen in the lane &
Moon witches in the woods.

I will make spicy cake
Pouring whiskey into its veins,
The shelves must creak with plenty
To keep out the dark &
Stop the sun slipping over the edge.

I will ladle out hot wine,
The glasses will scald your hands,
As the mists swirl up from the sea
Keep the fire higher, keep up the lights
Bring in the green branches.

Old gods are stirring under the mud
Stir, stir, with the pudding spoon,
Muttering incantations,
Dropping the silver in,
A wish, a wish.

The house hunches her shoulders,
Wink-eyed at the ghosts,
Clasping her shirt to her knees,
Feet curled under
The cat waits at the window.

Ring out the bells in the midnight.
Blind drunk in the pub, singing loudly
To keep the spirits away.
The crackers blast, eat large
And light the flaming tree.

We drowned death in our martinis,
Set a match to the dark,
Tight bellied we laugh with the brave,
The devil is frightened of my paper hat &
The sun is an orange balloon.

AUDREY SCALES (1933 —)

Born Northern Ireland, educated England, the Irish Republic
and at Queen's University, Belfast. Worked for a number of
years in London and the Middle East. Now married and lives
in Limavady. She says of her first collection, *The Ephemeral
Isle*, Limavady: Portmoon Press, 1983, that she hopes her
work will appeal to everyone, whether or not they normally
read poetry.

IRIS

Regal purple rises from a clutch of swords:
A chalice, a triumvirate of minuscule beards;
Velvet robe embroidered with a swarm of bees,
Emblem of France, the fleur-de-lis.

Yellow flags are out in meadow marshes
By the alder-dark river, lighting up the rushes;
The Light of the North — once Ireland's reputation,
Brief as a dragonfly's gossamer scintillation.

THE SNORE

The triffle, the squiffle,
The trumpet involuntary,
The tentative tremor,
The full-fledged roar;
The gargle, the bubble,
The rise and fall commentary,
The garbled murmur,
The all-night snore.

The waffle, the sniffle,
The night documentary,
The grunt, the whimper,
The unfeline purr;
The gasp, the chuckle,
The snort supplementary,
The audible dreamer,
The eight-hour bore.

THE RETURN TO LONDON

Interminable escalator —
How many more bras and briefs
Do we have to endure?

The affluent society
Gives me a pain.
It gives itself a pain too:
Grey faces grooved with anxiety
Are hurrying, trying, buying,
Straining in the dripping rain.

Take me back to the sun
To smiling faces
Where the old are cared for,
Where the issue is not underwear
But one thing to wear;
Not what shall we eat
But shall we eat today;
Not which car, but bare feet.

JOAN TRODDEN KEEFE (1930s –)

Born Co. Kildare, educated at University College, Dublin,
and University of California at Berkeley, where she now
teaches, but she spends the summers in County Cork. Gaelic
scholar and poet she is co-editor of *The Penguin Book of
Women Poets* (1978). Other publications are *The Other Voice*,
an anthology of contemporary women's poetry in translation,
New York: Norton, 1976, and (as translator and arranger)
Irish Poems: from Cromwell to the Famine, a miscellany,
Lewisburg: Bucknell University Press, 1977. Her poems,
articles and translations from the Irish have appeared in *The
Irish Press, The Kilkenny Magazine, The Journal of Irish
Literature, Soundings, New Orleans Review, The Nation,
World Literature To-day, Aisling* (San Francisco). She regu-
larly gives readings in the San Francisco Bay area and on local
radio. Keefe has made some valuable suggestions for the Gaelic
content of this anthology.

PICA PICA

Posed in a cool trellis of hedge shadow
This boulevardier of the boreen
Signals crossed thumbs against the sorrow
His single presence brings, a Byzantine

Bit of superstition. Studied elegance
Of jazzy gentleman-thief engaged to dance
A foxtrot while spiriting from glassy nitwits
Festoons of pearls, is a convincing switch

Of parts, still tradition upholds leisure
In his raffish geodesic dome;
Never stooping to slumming in the beeches

He assures our double joy and his own pleasure
By maintaining in unbroken sequence
The pick of Lady Picas in his home.

HACKETT'S HEAD

A bloody sample, Hackett's head was raised
Impaled on a stake before a crowd in Wicklow,
Denied the healing earth, though winter's fringe of snow
Muffled the noisy change of flesh to dust.

Raked by March winds, the bleakly emerging skull
Hail-scoured, rain-washed, joining the general
Rank of the common dead, housing no more sins,
Became an empty dome of spirals. Wrens,

Curious, flew in and out of Hackett's eyes,
Established a dwelling, liking lofty views.
When snapping eggshells splinter in his brain
The din of small birds sings through the bone like wine.

MARY FROST (1936 –)

Born Cork, educated St Aloysius School and University College (BA English and History), married in 1964 and has four children. She normally lives with her family in Oranmore, Co. Galway, but they have recently spent several years in Thunder Bay, Ontario. The two poems chosen here come from *The Salmon* (Galway) 5, Autumn 1982.

HAWTHORN

A three day gale has stripped the trees,
And whipped the ragged leaves

Back from the grass,
To huddle in hollows under the hedge;
Laid bare the beech and ash,
Stood out the hawthorn in conspicuous disgrace
All thorns and scarlet sins.

126

Poor ragged hawthorn stands beside the road,
A painted jezebel, a hedgerow whore,
Her guilt proclaimed by her ill-gotten gains,
Compelling condemnation like the poor satins.
Hostile receives
Starling and crows
And any tattered stray
That comes her way.

Retort

I'll hear no ill of hawthorn whom I knew
In the first blossom of her country youth.
Before the winds deflowered her she was fair
As anything that I've seen, anywhere.

RAIN SHOWER

The dry spell ended in a sudden outburst
Taking the garden chairs by surprise
Sluicing the roof-tiles
Punishing the dry presumption
Of laggard laundry lines
Set the crisp leaves
Muttering in tongues
And in the moment of its dissolution
    Inspired the dying dust.

MARY STANISTREET (1940 –)

Born Dublin 1940, educated Ursuline Convent, Waterford.
Took a BA Hons in English Literature and Classical Civilisa-
tion in Trinity College in 1985 as a mature student. Divorced,
she has four children and now lives in America. Her short
stories have been published in Great Britain, Holland, Norway
and Denmark and her articles in the Irish national press. She
is currently working on a novel.

ALKIE

She wails like a banshee,
Crying for drink.
And uses pseudonyms
Pain, fear, loss, courage, respectability.
Anything but its true face.

She pleads
'Let me die'
(In her own fashion she means)

Curled up in some gutter,
Drowned in the smell, taste, texture of a Smirnoff houri.
The stalemate stench of vomit clotted to her clothes.

She holds a towel between her legs,
Not that there is any blood to rise like sap,
But just to stop the urine flow she can't control
And sometimes, in a last great aged thrust
Spouts viciously on proper places like her drawing room floor.

She likes to see them mop it up, her daughters.
Their noses curled, distaste sown in the down curve of their lips.
They hate her noisesome dutiful smell.

They hide her bottles.
Cancel her cheques.
If they but knew it
She has a catholic taste
And would be happy with 70 proof piss.

'Conduct yourself' they say,
As if she were a symphony orchestra or a lightening bolt.
They don't know what it's like.
They can't cut down on cigarettes
Or walk a block
Or squeeze their pampered bodies
Into a size ten dress.

Nothing fat or sluggish about her body.
Whittled like a crow she is and
Tortured with need.
Sturdy too.

She'll outlive them all.
Spend the best years of their lives swilling merrily
In the deepest corner of the deepest hole
And, only come out when she wants.

THE SECRET

There are things about her
You would not like to know.

So, she doesn't tell you
And wonders,
Would it have made any difference
If you had known
That she let them suck
Your child from her body
With a long black tube.

128

She watched it being done.
His steady foreign eyes
Above the mask intent
On burrowing between her legs.

Everything seemed green.

The scrubbed walls, floor tiles,
Lights and theatre gowns.
Even the nurse
That stroked her brow
Was green.
Irish, and bellyful with child.

The ironies.

They told her step by step,
It would be less of a pain they said
To know what they were about.

But no one mentioned
The terrible hurt of loss.
The wound that dragged on
like the blood
For month upon mournful month.

Could she have told you this
Knowing it wouldn't matter?

CAITLÍN MAUDE (1941 – 1982)

Born Casla, Connemara, educated locally, at Mount Mellick
Convent and in Galway City. University College Galway Arts
degree. Taught Dundalk, Dublin, Castlebar, Co. Wicklow.
Married Cathal Ó Luain (1969), one son. Also worked as an
actress and singer of traditional songs. With her husband
involved in setting up an Irish school in Tallaght. Active in
the Gaeltacht civil rights movement in the early '70s. Wrote
one play in Irish, *An Lasair Choille* (with Michael Hartnett).
There is a Gael Linn record (1975) of *Caitlín* singing folk
songs and reciting her own verse. Her poetry was published
in *Comhar, Cyphers* and other periodicals. It was collected
and published after her death, *Caitlín Maude, Dánta* (ed.
Ciarán Ó Coighligh), Dublin: Coiscéim, 1984. 'Aimhréidhe'
was published in *NuaFhilí* 3, (1979) and 'Treall' in *NuaFhilí*
2. Some of her work is in *The Bright Wave/An Tonn Gheal:
Poetry in Irish Now*, Dublin: Raven Arts Press, 1986, the first
major anthology of Irish poetry translated into English.

AIMHRÉIDHE

Siúil, a ghrá,
Cois trá anocht —
Siúil agus cuir uait
na deora —
éirigh agus siúil anocht

    ná feac do ghlúin feasta
    ag uaigh sin an tsléibhe —
tá na blátha sin feoite
agus tá mo chnámhasa dreoite . . .

    (Labhraim leat anocht
    ó íochtar mara —
    labhraim leat gach oíche
    ó íochtar mara . . .)

Shiúileas lá cois trá
shiúileas go híochtar trá —
rinne tonn súgradh le tonn —
ligh an cúr bán mo chosa —
d'ardaíos mo shúil go mall
gur ansiúd amuigh ar an domhain
in aimhréidhe cúir agus toinn
chonaic an t-uaigneas id shúil
'gus an doilíos id ghnúis

Shiúileas amach ar an domhain
ó ghlúine go com
agus ó chom go guaillí
nó gur slogadh mé
sa doilíos 'gus san uaigneas

TANGLED

Wander, my love
along the shore tonight —
wander and stop
your weeping —
rise up and wander tonight
bend your knees no more
at that mountain grave —
those flowers are withered
and my bones are mouldering . . .
I speak to you tonight
from sea-depth —
I speak to you every night
from sea-depth . . .

I once wandered along the shore
I wandered to shore-end —
wave made game with wave —
white foam licked my feet —

slowly seeping into my vision
there out in the depths
in the tangle of foam and wave
I saw the loneliness in your eyes
and the sorrow in your face

I wandered out in the depths
from knees to waist
and from waist to shoulders
until I was swallowed
in sorrow and loneliness

(Translation: Joan Trodden Keefe)

TREALL

Tabhair dom casúr
nó tua
go mbrisfead is
go millfead
an teach seo,
go ndéanfad tairseach
den fhardoras
'gus urláir de na ballaí,
go dtiocfaidh scraith
agus díon agus
simléir anuas
le neart mo chuid
allais . . .

Sín chugam anois
na cláir is na tairní
go dtóigfead
an teach eile seo . . .

Ach, a Dhia, táim tuirseach!

CAPRICE

Hand me a hammer
or an axe
That I may break and
that I may wreck
this house,
that I may reduce the
lintel to a doorstep
and the walls to floors,
that scraws
and roof and
chimney
may come crashing down
as a result of my labours . . .

131

Pass me the boards and the nails now
that I may build this other house . . .

But, dear God, I'm tired!

(Translation: P. Riggs)

KATHLEEN O'DRISCOLL (1941 –)

Born Cork, degree in English/French/Italian from University
College, Galway, and higher diploma in education. Has worked
at various jobs and as a language teacher. From 1977 became
fulltime writer. Reads in schools under the Arts Council
Writers in Schools Scheme, has been published in Irish news-
papers and periodicals and broadcasts over RTE. She hopes
to continue writing on political, satirical and personal themes.
Publications include: *Goodbye Joe* (poems) 1980, and *Ether*
(short stories) 1981, both published Dublin: Caledon Press.
She is currently working on a novel. The two poems chosen
here are both uncollected.

THEOCRATS

A girl sold her body
To the custodians of our morality
Because they swore it was the only way
She could experience the joys of womanhood.
But she refused to include her soul in the bargain
And they said she was dishonest and unfeminine.

Finding, then, that she did not like
The tasks they expected of her body,
She saved like mad to buy her body back.
'But,' said the custodians,
When she asked them to reverse the bargain,
'You are not a member of our club
So your money is no good to us.
And besides, when we bought your body
We gave it to God,
And no one may ever ask things back from Him.'

'But, who is God?' she said,
'I can't make out
Whether He is your conservative statesman,
Your mediaeval churchman
Or your avaricious lawman.'
'You Infidel!
Our God is Three-In-One,' they said,
'And one questions God at one's peril!'
So, at dead of night
The girl snatched her body back from God.

'You have sinned grievously,'
Said the custodians of our morality.
'You must repent at once, or you will never get
Inside the gates of heaven.'
'To hell with heaven, honourable gentlemen,' said she;
'My freedom and the joys of life are good enough for me.'

MOTHERLAND

So long, my mystic land of milk and honey,
Beefy bankers, trendy lawyer-landlords,
Faultless pedigreed, god fearing killers exchanging
Tory blue for tory green.
You plump complacent sow
Devouring your fat farrow
While you shed the half-dead weak ones
On your neighbour, your own life long enemy,
Whom you blackmail to feed them on her scraps
Or else you'll tell the world of her dire meanness.

You think I'll quit your misty shores
In loving tears, forget my terror of your greedy henchmen,
Sing romantic ballads of your legendary beauties,
And perhaps return to die among your saints and heroes?

You puffed up, arrogant bloodsucker,
If I survive no thanks to you,
I'll show each soul I meet
My shrunken twisted heart
And give you credit
For your economic artistry.

ROÍSÍN COWMAN (1942 –)

Born Cork, and now lives in Co. Waterford. BA and higher
diploma of education from University College, Cork. Taught
French in schools in Ireland and Nigeria. Married with three
children. Now teaches part-time. 'Medea Ireland', chosen here,
was published in *The Adultery and other stories and poems*,
Maxwell House Winners 3, Dublin: Arlen House; London:
Marion Boyars, 1982. 'Dionysia' has not been published before.
Won Patrick Kavanagh Award in 1985.

MEDEA IRELAND

Snake mother at the psyche's core,
she uncoiled for him;

133

and by what power could she then
mate and breed
with one, who shook the island
with hell-thunderings from his book?

and with his lore of God's love
dying between thief and thief
and God's love living in a triple leaf
spread madness with his seed?

The rime of death on children's bodies still
delays his pursuit of her flight through time.

DIONYSIA

We do wrong,
to stop each outlet.
Public executions,

trips to Bedlam
where the madmen caper,
wars in Vietnam,

bull baiting, hares
dismembered, all
release us, give us air

The real circuses
are over now;
the blood-stained sand is swept
from the arena.

Only some clowns
remain in mimic rut
upon a lighted stage,
to still this rage

within the gut.

EILÉAN NÍ CHUILLEANÁIN (1942 –)

Born Cork, where her father was a professor of Irish. Her mother is Eilis Dillon, novelist and children's writer. Educated at University College, Cork, and at Oxford. Since 1966 lecturer in English at Trinity College, Dublin. Married to Macdara Woods, the poet, one son. Her poetry has been widely published in Ireland, Britain and the United States. Her first volume, *Acts and Monuments*, Dublin: Gallery Books, 1972, won the Patrick Kavanagh Award. She has since published *Site of Ambush* (1975), *The Second Voyage* (1977), *The Rose Geranium* (1981), all from Gallery Books. She is editor of *Cyphers* (Dublin) in which she said, (No. 10, Spring 1979, pp. 47-51), '. . . my own idea of the value of poetry is that it is a more precise form of expression than any other'. She has recently edited *Irishwomen: Image and Achievement*, Dublin: Arlen House, 1985. 'Wash' comes from *Acts and Monuments* and 'Ardnaturais' from *Site of Ambush*, both published by The Gallery Press.

WASH

Wash man out of the earth; shear off
The human shell.
Twenty feet down there's close cold earth
So clean.

Wash the man out of the woman:
The strange sweat from her skin, the ashes from her hair.
Stretch her to dry in the sun
The blue marks on her breast will fade.

Woman and world not yet
Clean as the cat
Leaping to the windowsill with a fish in her teeth;
Her flat curious eyes reflect the squalid room,
She begins to wash the water from the fish.

ARDNATURAIS

The steel edge of water shuts
My close horizon, shears off
Continents and the courses of ships.
An island in a saucer of air
Floats in the tight neck
Of the bay, sealing
An intimate coastline. No pounding historical waves,

No sandribbed invasions flung
At high tide on beaches
Or violent ebb sucking pebbles away.

Warm death for a jellyfish, lost
Ten legs in a crinoline; the furred bee
Slants down from the cliff field, straying
Over salted rocks. The water
Searches the branching algae and my hair
Spreads out like John the Baptist's in a dish.
Shouldering under, I feel fear
As I see them plain: the soft anemone,
Bladdered weed, the crouched spiked urchin, rooted
In one clutch of pebbles, their long strands
Shivering under the light.

Alone in the sea: a shallow breath held stiffly:
My shadow lies
Dark and hard like time
Across the rolling shining stones.

PATRICIA McCARTHY (1944 –)

Born Cornwall, educated Holy Child, Killiney, and Trinity
College, Dublin. Spent the formative years of her life in Ireland,
but now lives in Sussex. She has also lived in London, Washing-
ton, Paris and Bangladesh. Married. Has published *Survival*,
Washington: Lovejoy Press, 1975, and *A Second Skin*, Corn-
wall: Harry Chambers/Peterloo Poets, 1985. Her work has
appeared in *The Irish Times, New Irish Writing, Hibernia,
Broadsheet, The Dublin Magazine, Agenda, English, Cyphers*,
etc. She is working on a novel. 'Love-child' was published in
A Second Skin.

CONTEXTS

I'd have gone on wearing an apron
when you laid out rabbits and fish
at my feet, could we have stepped
behind our century of machines

and pills, with your body a scythe
and bulldozer, your hands trowels
that dug up groceries like treasure.
Yes, I'd have kept the fire going

in our hearts while you faced storms
to find birds' pickings, and prized
damp bits of kindling more
than exclusive french perfume.

I'd have been the most versatile
kitchen utensil with the supermarket
of the whole earth outside our door
and only our lives in our purses.

Your sweat would have broken out
upon my brow as I defined myself
by denials for tiny harvesting palms.
I'd gladly have hung our eyes' bulbs

from every ceiling and have washed
potatoes for part of my lore
in the bucket slopping over with water
you divined; our evening outing

a jaunt to see the corn sprouting
on the land's dark screen, better
than any cinema. A witch doctor —
I'd have delivered descants

from my groans on yearly childbeds
while you polished your sword for me —
and have wished for no other knight
than yourself. I need you still

to excavate airraid shelters
and carry my cases from your world
as I journey, unguided, into my own —
towards an indivisible beyond.

Blinded by fluorescent lighting
in skies, we no longer rise and fall
like bread together — but clatter
across concrete malls, apart.

LOVE-CHILD

Child whom I'll not carry,
I'd like you. You'd be a girl,
I think, a lefthanded knockout:
no sin, our only 'ours'.

He who'll never be your father:
one of three, three in one —
is kind and wouldn't insult you
with condemnation. The cradle

of his smile rocks beautifully —
with rowan leaves to protect you
from evil and abracadabras
in its corners in tiny triangles.

137

I've slid and slid down his body
arching over me your rainbow,
testing it for safety. While we wring
birth from death, death from birth —

unfair on you, he doesn't know
I've conceived you already
by embracing a May tree and
Saint Swithin swells me like an apple

with the rain. You can perch
on his palm, a Thumbelina,
as I fashion a caul from my webs
that will give you lyres —

so it's said and lovers
for the choosing. I'm avoiding
strawberries in case of markings
and touching wood for you

at every boasting. You need
more advantages than most.
You thrill my belly over all
the humpbacked bridges I cross

to him too fast, wavering
between desire and sense, instinct
and science. If I told him now,
he'd polish an eagle-stone

for me to wear on my arm,
rattling the pebble inside it
to make you squirm, doting as much
as me. But on the verge of you

I delay, withholding drams
of spit, sperm, wine and word
to mix with your squandered flesh
into a flying ointment

for saturnalia with you —
after the french-letter, worn
delicately as a caul, thrusts
at you the tenderest No.

As hens crow in the dark, eating
their eggs, I twist our last straw
of ecstasy into a harvest-baby
and I swaddle it in oblivion.

Author's notes:
The 'abracadabras' in 'triangles' refer to an ancient charm called the Sator. Abracadabra was sometimes written in a magic triangle to help the woman deliver.
It was an old belief that embracing a May-tree could cause a woman to conceive. (Golden Bough)
A baby born with a 'caul' was lucky. It was kept carefully as an amulet, and its owner gifted with eloquence, lovers and protected from drowning.
Strawberries, if craved during pregnancy, were meant to cause birth-marks on the unborn infant.
The 'eagle-stone' prevented abortion and eased birth. It was fastened to the arm and then to the thigh at the time of birth to attract the child into the world and prevent pain. It was a hollow stone, with a pebble in.
The 'flying ointments' belonged to witches. They made them from the fat of newly-dead infants, mixed with poplar leaves and soot, bat's blood, herbs etc. They produced illusions – of banquets etc. that they attended. Here the 'ointment' is pertinent because the whole idea of the 'love-child' is an illusion.
'Crowing hens' were meant to have the devil in them and really did eat their own eggs (having undergone a sort of sex-change). They were a sign of death.
It was an old harvest custom (pagan) to twist (and plait) the last sheaf of corn into a corn-dolly or harvest-baby. Other figures were formed also, depending on the region. This baby was meant to contain the spirit of the corn and to keep it alive for the next year.

EAVAN AISLING BOLAND (1945 –)

Born Dublin, the daughter of a diplomat, and a painter (Frances Kelly). Educated in London, New York, Holy Child, Killiney, and at Trinity College, Dublin, then lectured there (1967-8). Married to Kevin Casey, the novelist, two daughters, lives Dublin. She is a member of the Irish Academy of Letters. In 1968 she was awarded the Macaulay Fellowship in poetry. Her poetry has been published widely in Ireland, in British and American periodicals, and in anthologies. Her verse has been recorded for Harvard University. Her published volumes include: *New Territory*, Dublin: Allen Figgis, 1967; *The Warhorse*, London: Gollancz, 1975; *In her own image*, Dublin: Arlen House, 1980; *Night Feed*, Dublin: Arlen House, London: Marion Boyars, 1982; *The Journey*, Manchester: Carcanet Press, Dublin: Arlen House, 1986.

A SOLDIER'S SON
(for Andrew)

A young man's war it is, a young man's war,
Or so they say and so they go to wage
This struggle where, armoured only in nightmare,
Every warrior is under age –
A son seeing each night leave, as father,
A man who may become an ancestor.

In a backstreet stabbling, at a ghetto corner
Of future wars and further fraticide,
Son of a soldier who saw war on the ground,
Now cross the peace lines I have made for you
To find on this side if not peace then honour,
Your heritage, knowing as I do

That in the cross-hairs of his gun he found
You his only son, and when he aimed
And when the bullet cracked, the only sound
Was of his son rifling his heart. You twist
That heart today; you are his killed, his maimed.
He is your war; you are his pacifist.

THE GORGON CHILD

I

It was the dark month
when ice delivers from the earth
crocus by quick crocus
snow's afterbirth.

I wove under the lights
my lace of sweat.
Lifted, I looked down
at the snaky wet

my legs beheaded,
the slick, forked tongues
of your head
and for a glance

I petrified with the season.
Little gorgon
how you marrowed stone
into me,

the bitter truth
that giving birth
was our division.
A skull cap

of forceps cauled
the python stings,
the ringlet coils.
I lay back

to a cluck of nuns,
to a stone knowing:
from now our meetings
would be mere re-unions.

140

II

I start awake
from a soft sleep,
from a dream of heels
under my heart.

You are somewhere else,
weeping the jungle language
of new hungers.
I am stone again.

The milk heats.
The bottle warmer
ticks itself off.
I lift you up.

You suck busily.
By the mercy
of the nursery light
we grow less apart,

among bears and rag dolls,
in their big shadows
we flesh
to warm fact.

Light contracts.
The world lives down
the dark
union of its wonders.

The milkman hums away
to his doorsteps,
his empties.
You smile

at the swinging tails
and cardboard whiskers
of the cat mobile.
Dawn sunders

to define:
As you are my horizon,
I your earth,
I cradle you and see

how by separations
love survives
its own stone hour,
its gorgon birth.

ELIZABETH PEAVOY (1945 –)

Née Walsh, born Bective, Co. Meath, daughter of William Walsh and the writer, Mary Lavin*. Married with three children, she has lived in Mauritius with her family. They are now in Brussels. Her verse has been published in the *Cork Review*, and in *Cyphers*. 'Elegy Creole Child' is from *Cyphers* 15, (1981).

ELEGY CREOLE CHILD

Presque tout le monde est mort
all of the babies
fathers invalided, first brothers
threadbare uncles,
booted stand on the broken verge
a graveside where almost everyone is dead

A little creole child
would not withstand ignorance or myth
of science, whose hot art cannot spare
his flight mourant,
a den of black unhappy arms
can cradle a creole child

late for serum or massage to save,
not favoured
father makes shoes
mother makes shoes, and shoes
longing for her living boy.
So many mauritian journeys these shoes

will undergo,
working to replace the soles of all mauritius
side by side on the low workbench,
with leather that will not freely crack tear
slip, let-in nor falter
in this murky mauritian sun.

CATHERINE BYRON (1947 –)

Born London of an English father and Co. Galway mother. Lived Belfast 1948-64, but completed her education at Oxford. MA plus MPhil in medieval English studies. Has two daughters. Now lives Leicester, from where she freelances as a reviewer and teacher of creative writing. Travels in Ireland regularly. She started to write poetry again in 1979 while on a solitary camping trip in Donegal. In 1984 was awarded an East Midlands Arts (UK) major bursary. Her first collection is *Settlements*, Durham: Taxus Press, 1985, 1987. *Samhain*, a fourteen-poem sequence based on the 'Wasting sickness of Cuchulain', was broadcast on RTE in 1986 and published as a Taxus/Aril chapbook in 1987. Her second collection, *Turas*, will be published in 1988 by Taxus Press. 'The Black and Tans deliver her cousin's son' was published by *Poetry Ireland Review*, and 'Churching' by *Lines Review*; both poems are also in *Settlements*.

THE BLACK AND TANS DELIVER HER COUSIN'S SON –
Galway 1921

'Didn't she step out into the yard
God love her
and see her own son's brains
scattered like mash about the flags?
And didn't she then kneel down
and gather the soggy shards
of her womb's child into her apron
carefully, as a girl gathers
mushrooms in the September fields?
And didn't she then stifle
the outbreath of her grieving
till only a whistle
or whimper of her lamentation
was heard in that place lest
the soldiers note her tne more?'

CHURCHING
Her daughter in England is delivered of her first child –
Birmingham 1938

The church clanks empty after late Mass.

Returned from the far country of caring
and giving suck, she walks softly
to the familiar altar rails.

143

She notes the gew-gaw fleur de lys
her eye grown critical investigating
the pale and curling fronds
of her child's astonishing extremities.

She awaits the priest in an attitude
of humility, mantilla veiling
her amazement at sameness in this place only
amongst a world newmade
by her act of making.
Through the fingers of attempted prayer
she summons the hosanna tree
of the dawn of her delivery,
the sparrows' and starlings' gloria.
She hears the priest hurry
in cassock and crossed stole
from sacristy to sanctuary
and prepares her spirit for the spell
that will pronounce her
clean.

LINDA ANDERSON (1949 –)

Born Belfast, of a working-class Protestant family. Studied
French and Philosophy at Queen's University, and then took
a diploma in education. In 1972, she went to London, taught
French in a boys' school, worked in libraries and offices.
After the publication of her first novel, *To Stay Alive*, Lon-
don: Bodley Head, 1984; New York, 1985, she started working
full-time as a writer, helped by an Arts Council bursary and
an advance from her American publisher. Linda says she began
to write 'obsessed and distressed by the pain endured by the
Northern Irish, seeking to understand it.' In 1986, her second
novel, *Cuckoo*, was published by Bodley Head and she was
chosen as one of Top Ten new authors in a joint W.H. Smith
and *Cosmopolitan* promotion. The poem chosen here comes
from *Cyphers*, 10, Spring 1979.

GANG-BANG, ULSTER STYLE

Broken Belfast Street,
Grey and dingy,
Sealed off with barbed wire
To stop murderous neighbours.
You lived in that trap,
Suffocating.
He was in another prison
Called Long Kesh.

Sleepwalking woman,
You shuttlecocked
From jail to jail
On dutiful visits,
Your eyes were old
They did not match
The bright hair
That made men watch you
Avidly.

You met him —
Another starved somnambulist.
Two living corpses clung together,
Thawed each other for a while.
But they found out.
They dragged you to their playroom.
Now you lie limp,
Face down,
Dumped in a ditch.
Routine policemen come
Accustomed, stony-faced.
'Turn her over, see the damage'.

O, poor adventuress —
In the name of virtue,
They cut your flaxen hair,
Defiled your lovely breasts,
Before degutting you.

MEDBH McGUCKIAN (1950 –)

Born Belfast, educated Dominican Convent and at Queen's University. Writer-in-Residence at Queen's University. Married, three sons. Won the British National Poetry Society competition in 1979, an Eric Gregory Award (1980), the Rooney Prize (1982) and the Alice Hunt Bartlett Award (1983). Her work has appeared widely in Ireland, Britain, the USA and in France. It has been broadcast over Radio Ulster, and Radio 3 of the BBC, and has also appeared in many anthologies such as Gerald Dawe's *The Younger Irish Poets*, Belfast: Blackstaff, 1982, and *The Penguin Book of Contemporary British Poetry* (1983). Her collections include *Single Ladies*, Budleigh Salterton: Interim Press, 1980; *Portrait of Joanna*, Ulsterman Publications, 1980; *The Flower Master* (1982), followed by *Venus and the Rain* (1984), both Oxford & New York: Oxford University Press. McGuckian derives her main inspirations from female experience. Poems chosen here come from *Single Ladies*.

FAITH

My grandmother led us to believe in snow
As an old man in the sky shaking
Feathers down from his mattress over the world.

Her bed in the morning was covered with tiny scales,
Sloughed off in the night from peeling skin;
They floated in a cloud

Of silver husks to the floor, or spun
In the open window like starry litter,
Blowing along the road.

I burned them in a heap, a dream of coins
More than Thérèse's promised shower of roses,
Or Virgil's souls, many as autumn leaves.

GATEPOSTS

A man will keep a horse for prestige,
But a woman ripens best underground.
He settles where the wind
Brings his whirling hat to rest,
And the wind decides which door is to be used.

Under the hip-roofed thatch,
The bed-wing is warmed by the chimney breast;
On either side the keeping-holes
For his belongings, hers.

He says it's unlucky to widen the house,
And leaves the gateposts holding up the fairies.
He lays his lazy-beds and burns the river,
He builds turf-castles,
And sprigs the corn with apple-mint.

She spreads heather on the floor
And sifts the oatmeal ark for thin-bread farls:
All through the blue month
She tosses stones in basins to the sun,
And watches for the trout in the holy well.

The poem makes reference to ancient Irish fertility customs. 'burns the river':
alters its course by setting fire to parts of the bank.

CHINOISERIE

The gardeners of the Summer Palace curl
The mauve chrysanthemum petals with chopsticks.

146

They make the peonies bloom for the Emperor's birthday
By burning fires along the terraces all night,
Their colours deepening from hill to shore
To seem as if they're fading.

Bells tied to the flowers in the Magnolia Grove
Vibrate to the eunuchs' shuffle.
Opium clippers float to the waterfront
The white tears of gashed poppy pods.
In the Hall of Peaceful Seas bronze animals
Spout the hours in the shell of the horseshoe stairs.

Edible dogs, the wine of the snow leopard,
Hang in the shops, the live birds
With their sewn eyes. In the evening
Elderly gents, their lily feet unbound,
Walk their canary cages — the dwarfed
Imperial lion guards the Emperor's sleeve.

IVY BANNISTER (1951 —)

Born New York, has lived in Ireland since the age of nineteen.
A graduate of Trinity College, Dublin, where she also obtained
her doctorate in 1978, she is Irish by adoption, married with
one child. She has worked as a teacher and journalist. She
awaits publication of her book on G.B. Shaw's female charac-
ters. Her poetry has been published in *The Irish Press, The
Cork Examiner, Icarus, Hibernia*, etc. She also writes short
stories, published in Ireland and Britain. Her poems have twice
been chosen amongst the winners of Maxwell House com-
petitions. She is now writing drama, and won the O.Z. White-
head playwriting award.

THE MOON-CHILD AND HER EARTHLY PARENTS

I. *The Father*

By the muted light
Of a spring-silver moon,
One venerable idealist,
Bewhiskered and high-minded,
In rigid pursuit of truth
And scientific recognition,
Studied privately to create a vaccine
In the event of a new plague.
When by chance he isolated a virus,
Thousands suffered and died.

Horrified by this corruption
Of purely reasoned intent,
He sought no reward
And kept the secret deep
In his iron-chambered idealist's heart.

II. *Mother and Child*

His woman, yellow-skinned and haggard,
Had a peg-leg and one glass eye,
And, of course, a beautiful mind.
They copulated by moonlight.
To them was born a miniature woman,
Perfect in every detail,
Only tiny, oh so tiny,
With finely chiselled features
And well-made hands and feet;
The throbbing moon rose full and orange bright.

III. *The Sins of the Father*

Because she was odd, they locked her —
Child of their sin, this doll woman,
This amber kernel of perfection —
In a dark warm closet
To grow like a hyacinth bulb;
Not a hair's breadth did she alter.
For twenty-five sterile years
Their moon-child waited
To show her pearly glowing face
To a curious, staring public.

IV. *Resolution*

When at last, the bolts undone,
The unlovely parents
Shoved her into a hard-edged sunshine
Where shyly, she melted,
Where eye-bald, she disintegrated
To the bumps and grinds of a ribald lover.

CLAIRR O'CONNOR (1951 –)

Born Limerick, educated at St Mary's Convent there. Graduate of University College, Cork and MA in education from St Patrick's College, Maynooth. Taught in London 1972-77. Returned to Ireland to teach in Limerick, and now in Dublin. Married to Kevin Honan, one son. Her prose and poetry has been published in Irish newspapers, and in Irish, British and American periodicals. She won prizes at the Doneraile and Allingham festivals for short stories and poems. Her play 'Getting Ahead' has been produced by the BBC, and she has had a story in the feminist collection *Mad and Bad Fairies*, Attic Press, 1987.

SNAKE EYE

1

Pyjamas, the first thing on the list
when they said hospital. You chose
the pattern yourself, whorls of snakes
in blue-greens, intricate.

I packed your bag crushing
the pyjamas under apples and books.
In pyjamas I do not know you.

In bed I wake.
The moon threads the curtains,
the brasseyes of the bed stare.
The dream-serpent wakes me.

2

In the leaves of the jungle –
gummy greenness.
Netted against mosquitoes,
I watch the snake's guerrilla

colours slide from under the Virgin's
foot. No. I will not move the net
to look. In the fabric of your pyjamas,
in the cross-hatching of my skull,
he has found a home.

3

In sudden winter
the house lies
down in snow.

Fear slouches off
his skin and lodges
in my eye sockets;
the guest, shifteyed
ophidian, secures
his habitation.

MY MOON-RED CLOCK

Luminous, white as bone
my anger; the creeping
Virginia bloodies stone
walls and a dying time
of year is called beautiful.

This venetian blind
stripes my moon-dragged
body in its red flow.

No longer mystified
by the butcher's
apron, I watch him carve
and cut to order —
admire his red display.

My blood-tears tick
new time, spotted moon.
I do not want this
insolent colour but
the white of pearls.

———————

NUALA NÍ DHOMHNAILL (1952 –)

Born in England where her Gaelic Leaguer/surgeon father was
studying. Mother (from Ventry) also a doctor. Educated in
Nenagh, Co. Tipperary and at University College, Cork (BA
Irish/English, HDipEd). Lived in Holland and in Turkey,
where she taught English and started again to write in Irish.
Married to a Turkish geologist, three children. In 1980 an
Arts Council bursary enabled her to return to the Dingle
Gaeltacht and write full-time. First collection, *An Dealg
Droighin* (Cló Mercier, two editions) shared an Oireachtas
prize (1982) and won Arts Council Prize for Irish Poetry
1980-82. In 1983 moved to Dublin and second collection,
Féar Suaithinseach (Maynooth: An Sagart) published 1984,

won both Duais an Ríordánaigh and the special 'Gradam an Oireachtais'. She has two further poetry collections in preparation, and is also working on a play for children, and a play for adults. She writes only in Irish. Some translations by Michael Hartnett from her first collection have appeared in *Raven Introductions 3*, and Sean Dunne's *Poets of Munster*, Brandon/Anvil Press, 1985, and a further selection in *Selected Poems*, Dublin: Raven Arts Press, 1986. Nuala says she is now researching into folklore and mythological themes which will enable her to express herself in a natural and yet imaginatively suggestive Irish.

AG COTHÚ LINBH

As ceo meala an bhainne
as brothall scamallach maothail
éiríonn an ghrian de dhroim
na maolchnoc
mar ghine óir
le cur i do ghlaic,
a stór.

Ólann tú do shá ó mo chíoch
is titeann siar i do shuan
isteach i dtaibhreamh buan,
tá gáire ar do ghnúis.
Cad tá ag gabháil trí do cheann,
tusa ná fuil
ach le coicíos ann?

An eol duit an lá ón oíche,
go bhfuil mochthráigh mhór
ag fógairt rabharta,
go bhfuil na báid
go doimhin sa bhfarraige
mar a bhfuil éisc is rónta
is míolta móra
ag teacht ar bhois is ar bhais
is ar sheacht maidí rámha orthu,

go bhfuil do bháidín ag snámh
óró sa chuan
leis na lupadáin lapadáin
muranáin maranáin,
í go slim sleamhain
ó thóin go ceann
ag cur grean na farraige
in uachtar
is cúr na farraige
in íochtar?

151

Orthu seo uile an bhfuilir
faoi neamhshuim?
is do dhoirne beaga
ag gabháilt ar mo chíoch.

Tánn tú ag gnúsacht le taitneamh,
ag meangadh le míchiall.
Féachaim san aghaidh ort, a linbh,
is n'fheadar an bhfeadaraís
go bhfuil do bhólacht
ag iníor i dtalamh na bhfathach,
ag slad is ag bradaíocht,
is nach fada go gcloisfir
an 'fí-faidh-fó-fum'
ag teacht thar do ghuaille aniar.

Tusa mo mhuicín a chuaigh
ar an margadh,
a d'fhan age baile,
a fuair arán agus im
is ná fuair dada.
Is mór liom de ghreim tú
agus is beag liom de dhá ghreim,
is maith liom do chuid feola
ach ní maith liom do chuid anraith.

Is cé hiad pátrúin bhunaidh
na laoch is na bhfathach
munar thusa is mise?

SUCKLING THE CHILD

Out of the honey-mist of the milk,
out of the cloudy heat of the beastings
the sun rises from behind
the low-slung hills
like a golden guinea
to place in your hand
little baby.

You drink your fill from my breast
and then fall back, asleep
into an everlasting dream,
you wear a little smile.
What's going on in your head?
you, who are only a fortnight alive.

Can you tell day from night?
Do you know that the low tide threatens
to turn to flood?

That the little boats are out on the deep
where fishes and seals and enormous whales
are dashing on the sides of the blades
and sweeping over the men at the oars
as they row

that your little boat
is floating, hóró, in the bay
with the splashing, floundering
little creatures of the sea, —
a smooth shapely vessel
from head to toe
bringing the gravel of the sea
above
and putting the foam of the sea
below?

You grunt with satisfaction
and give a foolish smile.
I look in your face, little baby
and wonder are you aware
that your sheep are in the meadow
your cows in the corn of the giants
ravaging and plundering
and that before long you will hear
the tune of fee-fair-fo-fum
sounding in your left ear.

You are my little piggy
that went to market
that stayed at home
that got bread and butter
and that got none.
I find you too big for one bite
and too little for two,
I like the smell of your flesh
but I don't like your broth.

And where have the
heroes and giants their origin
if not here with you and me?

(Trans. the author & P. Riggs)

OILEÁN

Oileán is ea do chorp
i lár na mara móire.
Tá do ghéaga spréite ar bhraillín
gléigeal os farraige faoileán.

Toibreacha fíoruisce iad t'uisí
tá íochtar fola orthu is uachtar meala.
Thabharfaidís fuarán dom
i lár mo bheirfin
is deoch slánaithe
sa bhfiabhras.

Tá do dhá shúil
mar locha sléibhe
lá breá Lúnasa
nuair a bhíonn an spéir
ag glinniúint sna huiscí.

Giolcaigh scuabacha iad t'fhabhraí
ag fás faoina gciumhais.

Is dá mbeadh agam báidín
chun teacht faoi do dhéin,
báidín fionndruine,
gan barrchleite amach uirthi
ná bunchleite isteach uirthi
ach aon chleite amháin
droimeann dearg
ag déanamh ceoil
dom fhéin ar bord,

thógfainn suas
na seolta boga bána
bogóideacha; threabhfainn
tri fharraigí arda
is thiocfainn chughat
mar a luíonn tú
uaigneach, iathghlas,
oileánach.

ISLAND

Your body is an island
in the middle of the great ocean,
your limbs spread out on a white sheet
as on a sea of gulls.

Your temples are wells of freshwater,
blood below, sweetness above.
They would cool me
in a fever,
they would be my healing potion
in illness.

Your two eyes
are mountain lakes
on a fine August day
when the sky sparkles in the pools.
Your lashes brush-like reeds
growing on their banks.

And had I a little boat
that would take me to you,
a white bronze boat
without the tip of a feather sticking out

154

or the end of a feather sticking in
but only one white-backed red feather
making music for me on board

I'd hoist up my soft white bellying sails,
I'd plough through the high seas
and I'd come to you
where you lie
lonely, greenmeadowed
as an island.

(Trans. the author & P. Riggs)

ELIZABETH MELLON (1954 –)

Born Dublin. Now lives in London. Her poetry has been published in *The Irish Times* and read on BBC Radio 4. 'Performance' was published in *Hibernia*.

PERFORMANCE

Under a chill torchlight
Steam ribbons smoke,
Encircling a swan.
Stark white
Funnels an image,
Spotlights a stage.
He performs an actor's ritual
With such swooning grace,
Curving ecstasy with ease,
That I think I see a swan.

Under a placid moon
His languid arch
Is a broken branch.
I caught a swan
In the act.

MARY E. O'DONNELL (1954 –)

Born Monaghan, educated St Patrick's College, Maynooth.
Now teaches at a Dublin secondary school. Her poetry has
been published in *Poetry Ireland, New Irish Writing, Cyphers,
The Honest Ulsterman, Tracks, The Salmon, Krino*; also in
the USA. She has given many poetry readings in Ireland, as
well as RTE broadcasts. A television series, 'The Poet's Eye',
in which she reads from her own work, is scheduled for
Autumn 1987 (RTE TV). She has won prizes for short stories
and poetry at Listowel Writers' Week and elsewhere. Her
stories have appeared in *The Irish Press*. 'Excision' has been
chosen here for its brave approach to a delicate subject.

EXCISION

She grapples in child innocence, mad
with hysteric hurt as the women hold
her down and bind with florid pain:
The cropping of pink lips, curling

coral from screaming girls. Rout
of beaded hyacinth, the weave and
cluster; maize-mornings scythed
by a midwife's halting swipe;

sources dammed like well cast
witchery, before dust days have
frisked in the sun's eye – the
sapping thrust of being honestly

alive: The brothers kick dust at
the sun, run like antelope beyond
the tent. Inside, a stitched stump,
a botched hole, pain that cannot

levitate beyond itself, fear of
woman's pleasure, blocked sun-tide of
the matriarchy, seeping fissures on the
dam wall. On it runs, riddles,

cutting the world's women: Razor
in Sudan, yashmak in Tehran,
purdah in India,
two tongues for Japan.*

Here, veiled tranquillity, the
splice and fever of diet and clean
hair, fragrance, spruce linen;
children, gleaming, scrubbed clones,

156

excised like her, the genie in
little heads mopped of mystery
till they too live a crisp anxiety.
Neither goddess nor woman inhabit

this temple for which earth is carved,
but diamond fortitude, covert moments
trickling to crows feet, gimlet eyes
which mirror sparkling smiles. It rots

the brightest soul until she
is too cuntless to dare, too numb
to snare the trancing of
voluptuous years that bled her

white and loathe to fight.
Her torpor fractures the wall.
Fissures creep. The sun-tide
rises even as she sleeps.

Razor in Sudan,
yashmak in Tehran,
purdah in India,
two tongues for Japan.

*In Japan, there's a male and female version of spoken Japanese: Males may use
both forms whereas females may use the female version alone.

NUALA ARCHER (1955 –)

Born New York, of Irish parents. She has lived in Latin, Central
and North America and – on and off since 1976 – in Dublin.
She has studied at Wheaton College, Illinois, Trinity College,
Dublin, the University of Wisconsin, Milwaukee, and the
University of Navarre, Pamplona. She is now teaching at
Oklahoma State University. Her work has been published in
Irish, British and American periodicals. Prizes won include a
First at Listowel Writers' Week and the Irish Distillers/Patrick
Kavanagh Award 1980. Her collection *Whale on the Line*, in
which both poems chosen here appear, was published Dublin:
Gallery Books, 1981. Editor of *Midland Review*, Winter 1986,
No. 3, a feature issue of Irish Women's Writing (Oklahoma
State University Press).

WHALE ON THE LINE
for John

1

You can't hear me dialling your number
because a whale is tangled
in the telephone cables on the ocean floor.
For some unknown reason

he torpedoed to the bottom. Cables entwine
the spool of his body — forty-five tons
of blubber the colour of your blue eyes.
His last air bubbles drift up

like small parachutes. He explores
the darkness by ear, listens
to kelp wave solemnly back and forth
like ushers at a funeral.

It took the scuba divers
days of overtime to unknot the mesh.
Arc lamps scattered light
in strange shadows. A white octopus

floated about, curling and uncurling
his arms like yo-yo's, gently touching
the whale's slack muscles,
open mouth and lidded eyes.

2

For months words drift in shoals
around the quiet whale . . . 'Remember
nightingales, stars, hibiscus, the late
train, willows of wind . . . ?'

Fish gargoyles, carrying lamps,
pick barnacles off the whale's back.
Submarine gulls circle and scream
Ballena! Ballena! Kujira! Kujira!

The whale's skull lies in sand.
A seaweed tongue flutters with the tide.
His stoney ears patiently become
the water sounding against a calf

just born to blue-green September
light. Soft explosions of breath
buoy her thermos-shaped body.
An albatross wraps the five-foot cord

around its neck, tears into placenta
as a clean wind tears clouds open.
Half-awake the calf rolls with the slanting
sea into a night brightened by the moon's

rainbow witches. Fog horns call back memories
of ships — *Union, Essex, Ann Alexander*
and *Kathleen* — sent to the bottom by whales;
and of whales lashed to my call of love for you.

DANCE OF WIND AND WASH

Unlike myself, there are women who do not lie
in bed every morning wondering: *Shall I get up?*
My mind roams capitals and anonymous
villages of the world and everywhere I see them
hanging out the most beautiful wash.

There is something about these women
and their lines of flowing shapes and colours
which prompts me from between sheets.
I get dressed and head north into where I am —
into the cold, clear light of the Pyrenees —
to photograph their laundry.

I pass hundreds of lines, each one distinct.
Some are taut and forthright, some relaxed
hung between trees or just outside windows.
The lines are their own horizons —
humming cables transmitting the glare of light.

Clothes are held to the lines by brown
or coloured pegs — bibs, bras and blouses,
blankets twisting into knots,
blue and pink striped sheets puffing
into spinnakers, nylons dancing, shoes hanging
disconsolately by their laces.

The sound of these threaded syllables swaying
like white shadows, a splayed deck of cards or arching
dolphins comforts me. I'm haunted
as much by the clothes as by bits of coastline
glimpsed between folds of bath towels.

I'm haunted too by your presence which hangs out
in my clothes, on my lines and whose ghostly
(and perhaps more substantial) swaying —
despite what seems a waste of lonely years —
I'm only now beginning to name.

159

ANNA-MARIA FLYNN (1955 –)

Born and raised in Belfast. Trained in Belfast as a nurse, but disliked this so moved to Dublin, working at various jobs. Her first poem was published in the *Irish Independent* (1977). In 1978 she published a small collection entitled *Lisowen*, subedited a short-lived literary magazine, did poetry readings in Mayo, Kerry, Dublin and Belfast, and broadcast recitations on RTE and various pirate radio stations. 'Wonder' is an unpublished poem; 'Into the Night' is included in her collection, *Inner Ports*, Dublin: Cillenna Press, 1981.

WONDER

Oh Greek God for which the Angels shied
time now sifts your memory
and leaves behind threads,
in some mongrel writing.
What of your beauty that brought the mass,
to kneel at your feet?
Begging for touching favours
Or the endless chants of praise
from new found lovers.
Are not we all lovers of paradise?
When grudging days fall upon us.
Oh give us back your tales and wonders
beyond the reams of mind.
Cast now your net, that elope with the corners of the world.
For time wearies with all young
the mirror reflects an older me
while I glance at older men.

INTO THE NIGHT

With a thunderstorm and a crooked snout
he went into the night
he cursed the rats and he cursed the folk
dipped his head, sneered their smile
'Give him five pence Jack'.

Cursed women with purple eyes
fleas between their fingers
'I'll piss a ring around them yet.'
The darling boys along on their pitiful wings.
Have a bowl of soup
I understand your complaint.
Read all about it
in Doctor Flamingo's book

your sort on a hook
come with me
give you a bath
and after that . . .
yeah . . . yeah . . . after that
have a scratch and bow my head to the kind, kind people.

Still —
makes them feel good and clean
snotters on a white-washed wall.
The crime that I commit —
I am seen picking the pride of man
pearly white teeth, nuclear power
superior intellectual race
tip-toeing across the sky of disinfectant clouds.
'Who said man descended from the apes?'
Man evolved from digital clocks
I suppose
I do humble society
so I fulfil a useful role in God's eternal plan
not only do I house nature's little ones,
I urinate perfume into the industrial air
my arse firmly to the ground I stand
as symbol from what thou art
my simple presence serves
to remind of the lack of achievement in
the scientific world.
My corroding teeth
knotted hair
prove the words of Christ
beyond a shadow of a doubt
'from dirt thou came, to dirt thou shall return'.
But I weary of spreading the gospel
to the unlightened
from the rising of the sun
till the hairy-arsed children go home
I beg for alms that my mission may be carried through
on a daily basis
a hard road, chasing sweaty couples from my skippering quarters
thus preserving purity
keeping the growth of the population at bay.
Walking back and forth along the flagstones
pointing the way to the energy crisis
But, who am I to boast?
Someday my humble wisdom shall shine through
a marble stone shall be erected to preserve my mortal appearance.

'Go on Jack, give him five pence.'

ÁINE NÍ GHLINN (1955 –)

Born Co. Tipperary, holds a degree in Irish from University College, Dublin (1976) and now teaches in Dublin. Her poetry has been published in *Inntí, Poetry Ireland, Cyphers, Comhar, An t-Ultach, Nua-Aois*, the *Sunday Independent*. She has also done readings for RTE (radio and television) and for Radio na Gaeltachta.

The poem she has chosen for this anthology is the title poem of her collection *An Chéim Bhriste*, Dublin: Coiscéim, 1984.

AN CHÉIM BHRISTE

Cloisim thú agus tú ag teacht aníos an staighre. Siúlann
tú ar an gcéim bhriste. Seachnaíonn gach éinne í ach
siúlann tusa i gconaí uirthi.

D'fhiafraigh tú díom céard é m'ainm. Bhíomar le chéile is
dúirt tú go raibh súile gorma agam.

Má fheiceann tú solas na gréine ag deireadh an lae is má
mhúsclaíonn sé thú chun filíocht a scríobh . . .
        Sin é m'ainm.

Má thagann tú ar cuairt chugam is má bhíonn 'fhios agam gur
tusa atá ann toisc go gcloisim do choiscéim ar an staighre . . .
        Sin é m'ainm.

Dúirt tú gur thuig tú is go raibh mo shúile gorm. Shiúil tú
arís uirthi is tú ag imeacht ar maidin.

Tagann tú isteach sa seomra is feicim ó do shúile go raibh
tú léi. Ní labhrann tú ná ní fhéachann tú ar mo shúile. Tá
a cumhracht ag sileadh uait.

Tá an chumhracht caol ard dea-dhéanta is tá a gruaig fada
agus casta. Cloisim thú ag insint di go bhfuil a súile gorm
is go bhfuil tú i ngrá léi.

Osclaím an doras agus siúlann tú amach.

D'fhéadfá é a mhíniú dhom a deir tú. Dúnaim an doras.

Ní shiúlann tú uirthi. Seachnaíonn tú an chéim bhriste. Ní
shiúlann éinne ar an gcéim bhriste. Déantar í a sheachaint
i gcónaí.

THE BROKEN STEP

I hear you coming up the stairs. You walk on the
broken step. Everyone avoids it but you walk on
it always.

You asked me my name. We were together and you
said I had blue eyes.

If you see the sunlight at the end of the day
and it awakens a poem in you . . .
            That is my name.

If you come to visit me and I know it is you
because I hear your footstep on the stairs . . .
            That is my name.

You said you understood and that my eyes were
blue. You walked on it again when you were leaving
in the morning.

You come into the room and I see in your eyes that
you were with her. You don't speak and you don't
look at my eyes. Her perfume flows from you.

The perfume is tall slender and well-formed and her
hair is long and curling. I hear you tell her that her
eyes are blue and that you love her.

I open the door and you walk out.

You can explain you say. I close the door.

You don't walk on it. You avoid the broken step.
Nobody walks on the broken step. They avoid it always.

                                (Author's translation)

163

PAULA MEEHAN (1955 –)

Born and raised in Dublin, educated Trinity College (BA) and
Eastern Washington University (Master in Fine Arts). She has
published very little but has read poetry frequently in Ireland
and the USA. She has worked for many years in the area of
community/political theatre in Dublin. 'T.B. Ward' comes
from *Return and No Blame*, 'Taking the Boat' is from *Reading
the Sky*, both collections published Dublin: Beaver Row
Press, 1984 and 1986.

T.B. WARD

The crows are holding court
Outside on the lawn. The one
In the centre is the spitting image
Of a vindictive old bitch
Who taught me Domestic Science
In a poxy convent in Finglas
When I was too young and stupid
To give the scaldy arse
A boot in the cunt and run.

The jerky consultant down the other
End of the ward leers at a gobshite
From Tuam. To listen to her you'd swear
She had a crucifix rammed up her hole.
The student doctors do a danse macabre
Exactly like a picture I once saw
In this rapid book about the Middle Ages
In the library ages ago of Trinity College:

Skeletons rattling down the street
Or else sticking out of wheelbarrows
That were parked all over the place.
I think it was Germany. The tea trolley
Trundles by. One lump. One lump, please.
The gorgeous black haired country nurse
Shells out my daily pills. Two blue, one red
And the long orange one. Over the aisle

The Kerrywoman rubs the holy picture
Of Padre Pio over her chest. Bagabones
She calls me. At night we sing hymns
For they're the only songs she knows
To go with the few bottles Jemmo smuggles in.
He keeps asking to play the Bard of Armagh
On my ribs. Slimy little fucker.
Up here on this pinnacle of self pity

The air is so thin, so frighteningly
Thin, that I fear my heart
Will explode in a million pieces.
Who could wake me from that cold?
The clumps of heather you brought
From Bray Head smell of the sea.
I've braided them into my hair.
How beautiful the diseased may appear
Rosy cheeked and glittery eyed!

　　Rings ringa rosy pocket full of poesy
　　Atisha atisha we all fall down.

Maybe it was a picture of Cronos:
Time eating his children,
Their little legs sticking
Out of his mouth as he scrunched
His way through the bones;
And not a wheelbarrow full of limbs
In that book on the Middle Ages
When I was a student ages ago.

TAKING THE BOAT

The bakers were on strike.
Sleeves rolled up she pounded
Dough viciously. She beat

The mound flat and sliced
Precisely with her old knife.
It might have been my heart she cut.

She formed the parts into smooth
Cobs. Outside in the blue a plane's
Wing caught the sun. 'Not even

A decent pair of shoes on your feet.
Nothing to your name. He'll have no time
For you once you're used goods. Measure

My words, girl.' She put the loaves to rise.
She held me to her breast. Under the fall
Of her hair I breathed her breath.

Later, a bar, Dun Laoghaire pier; in the mirror
I meet the eyes of my first lover.
He would teach me much about death.

165

SIOBHÁN CAMPBELL (1962 –)

Born and lives in Dublin and has University College, Dublin,
degree. Her poetry has been published in *The Irish Press,
Cyphers* and *Hard Lines 3*, ed. Tom Paulin, London: Faber
& Faber, 1987. 'Antrim Boarders' appeared in this last col-
lection. She is involved with the Dublin Writers' Workshop
and Voicefree, a Dublin writers group.

ANTRIM BOARDERS

We used to meet
behind the science lab
where you went to smoke
and I went to read.
You named me Red.

They voted me
boy most likely to succeed
three years in a row
but then you skipped a class
and won because the lads were afraid.

And when we were left in Belfast
to make our own way home
I slid in with the post on a train.
But you told some Republican Prod
that your granny was raped by a Brit
and arrived back in her model-T Ford
with your belly full of cream.

Once after science you showed
how you wore nylons
under your trousers
and I got a thrill.
Afterwards, I knew
you wouldn't meet me there again.

I've heard you are in London now
in a suit by day
and a skirt by night.
I wonder have you heard
that I am still called Red
or if you have guessed
that I never came out.

ROSITA BOLAND (1965 –)

Born in Ennis, Co. Clare and is a student in Trinity College, Dublin. Her work has appeared in *The Sunday Times, Cyphers, The Evening Herald* and the Faber anthology, *Hard Lines 3.* Her translations from the Irish of Cathal Ó Searcaigh appeared in *The Bright Wave*, Raven 1986 and a selection of her poems appeared in *Raven Introductions 4*, 1986 (from which 'Fireworks' is taken).

FIREWORKS

We sat with our arms held tight
Around each other
While we watched the fireworks blow open
In huge, coloured dandelion puffs
That burst and fell like melting tinsel
Against the backdrop of an August night.

I knew that those nights
Were climbing into bed beside us,
Staining the sheets with their dark colours
I kept reaching out for you,
But my arms were burning only in a night
That gathered me into an empty embrace
Until sliding quietly away into dawn,
Leaving its indigo shadows smeared
Beneath the ashy embers of my eyes.

That same year,
You tossed me away with the casual, easy grace
That came so fluidly to your deft hands
And sent me spinning through the Autumn
Exploding in savage reds and orange
That came too late to scald you.

SARA BERKELEY (1967 –)

Born in Dublin, a selection of her poems appeared in *Raven Introductions 3* in 1984 and her work has appeared in *Cyphers, The Irish Times, The Irish Press* and *The Evening Herald*. She contributed a number of translations from the Irish to the dual language collection of poems, *The Bright Wave*, Raven, 1986 and her first collection *Penn* from which 'Seeding' is taken, was also published by Raven in that year.

SEEDING

The shuttle works onwards from winter's backward draw
Springtide washing driftwood high on her sighblown beach
The woman waits, tight-limbed,
Time-dried, for her babies to begin.

Other circles weave revolving arcs into her day
Splitting a pea-pod – the tiny explosion
Of ripe, tense seeds, spiralling back along the wind-curved edge
The floating time seeds of the dandelion
And burdocks fuzz the grass, sycamore on a dizzy wing,
False fruits of her pangless labour.

A myriad of scattered grains
When the stamen bends with belly full
And swelling buds listen
To the easy breath of blood-veined leaf
In the rhythmic black-blue, black-blue night
And tenuous quivering light.

Wider circles weave their shadows on the earth
High on the brow, wind-dried, hardly bruised
With handling – the fruit of no rain.

Early morning draws water from the driest eyes
In crop and field, waiting woman drinks from thin air
Tasting dry in her mouth, the seed quiet
Deep in her virgin earth where winter leaves
The trees bare.

INDEX OF TITLES

172

INDEX OF CONTRIBUTORS